W9-AAH-656

Books by Donald Day

BACKWOODS TO BORDER

(*Edited with Mody C. Boatright: a Texas Folklore Society Publication*)

FROM HELL TO BREAKFAST

(*Edited with Mody C. Boatright: a Texas Folklore Society Publication*)

BIG COUNTRY: TEXAS

(*American Folkways Series*)

THE AUTOBIOGRAPHY OF WILL ROGERS

(*Editor*)

FRANKLIN D. ROOSEVELT'S OWN STORY

(*Editor*)

HOW WE ELECT OUR PRESIDENTS (by Will Rogers)

(*Editor*)

How We Elect Our Presidents

WILL ROGERS

How We Elect Our Presidents

SELECTED AND EDITED BY
DONALD DAY

Little, Brown and Company · *Boston*

LIBRARY OF CONGRESS CATALOG CARD NO. 52–5018

FIRST EDITION

Published simultaneously
in Canada by McClelland and Stewart Limited

PRINTED IN THE UNITED STATES OF AMERICA

To

Will Rogers, Jr.

Contents

How We Elect Our Presidents

Caucus

"Politics is the best show in America," Will Rogers said. "I love animals and I love politicians and I like to watch both of 'em play either back home in their native state or after they have been captured and sent to a zoo or to Washington."

But best of all Will loved the Presidential nominating conventions. He'd swear and he'd groan and he'd shout that he wasn't going to go to another one but every fourth year when that "political bunk" got into his nostrils he hopped the nearest plane and was there ahead of the preliminary maneuverings.

"Its one of the Follies we have built up that no other country could understand," he said, "but it has a fascination for us. Its the one place where our public men can do foolish things and due to the surroundings they look kinder plausible at the time. It takes weeks after one is over to see what was really inside it. Then is when our sense of humor asserts itself."

In this book Will reports the conventions from 1920 until his death in 1935, takes them apart after they are over, and then wryly describes some of the comedies (or tragedies) that unfold as a result of their doings. The peep he gives is of a world as different from today as our sleek convertibles are from a Model-T Ford. Yet the basic motivations and machinery are there and it is suspected that you might learn more truly what is going to happen at Chicago this year from what he said than from the contemporary reportings over radio, on television or in newspapers.

Old Will really stripped off the hide and showed what made Uncle Sammy run — or as he would say, misrun!

Most of this material was published in the New York Times *and sent out to hundreds of papers by the McNaught Syndicate. Some of it appeared in the* Saturday Evening Post *and on Gulf Oil Company's radio broadcasts. My thanks to them for permission to use it.*

Here he is with his lariat and his grin!

DONALD DAY

P.S.: The leaders of the Republican party can profit from what Will wrote on March 30, 1929, in the Saturday Evening Post. *The Democrats most assuredly should study his sage words of November 11, 1934.*

CHAPTER ONE

"Back to Normalcy"

World War I and the internationalist policy of President Woodrow Wilson had taken the United States a long mile from its traditional isolationism. Many people dreaded this move as a departure from George Washington's advice against "entangling alliances."

In true political tradition the party that was out — the Republican — took its stand against the position of the party that was in — the Democratic.

The Republicans snatched control of Congress in the off-year elections of 1918 and then grimly set about getting the Presidency also in 1920. As the time for the political conventions drew near it became more and more obvious that the issue would be whether to go into Wilson's League of Nations or to repudiate it.

The Republican's battle cry — "back to normalcy" — was based on the party's promise that the country would go its own way.

This was the political situation when Will Rogers first began to do "police reporting on our national political clambakes." The Republicans chose Chicago and the

Democrats settled on San Francisco as their respective meeting places.

Will was busy making a moving picture — Cupid, the Cowpuncher — *and could not attend in person. But he didn't let that bother him a bit. He reported them just the same.*

JUNE 2, 1920 [*before the conventions*]

I'm giving these conventions the absence treatment since I am out in California making a movie, *Cupid, the Cowpuncher*. But you don't have to hear somebody say a thing to know it. Why, I'll bet the typewriter — the machine, not the blond that runs it — which has lived through a convention or two just automatically run off all the speeches including the "applause" and "wild cheering for twenty minutes."

President Wilson says the old Testament stayed as it was written and he thinks the League of Nations had just as good authors as it did.

It will be considered an honor this year to be nominated by the Republicans but with the Democrats it will be considered a duty. They will meet this year through force of habit.

When Hoover decided to be elected on the Republican Ticket he picked the wrong party. He should have stayed with the Democrats where the opposition was not so keen. I guess he figured that it was better to be defeated for the nomination than to be a Democrat and then get defeated in the election.

Pres. Wilson is going to retire to Princeton University.

He says the pay may not be as plentiful but neither is the advice.

JUNE 4, 1920

Congress wants to abolish Slush Funds. Why, that distributes more money among the needy delegates than anything. Imagine a Congress that squandered 30 Billions trying to find out where some candidate spent a few thousand!

I have been asked to cover the Republican Convention, to write something funny. All you have to do to write something funny about a Republican Convention is just tell what happens.

The Convention is held in Chicago. Chicago is located just North of the U. S. I am well acquainted with the American Consul there. Chicago holds the record for Murders and robberies and Republican Conventions.

The Convention started off with a setback. A carload of wine billed for Chicago for "Medical Purposes" got held up.

The Democrats are investigating slush funds. If they can find where it come from they want theirs.

JUNE 9, 1920

I know who will be nominated but the Republican leaders have asked me not to tip it off as the hotels and other crooks in Chicago want to keep the suckers there a few days till they are thoroughly renovated.

They called in a Professional pray-er as none of the Politicians present knew how. Of course Bill Hays [*Re-*

publican National Chairman] has told him what to pray for. A great many of the leading Republicans were against having the Prayer as they didn't think it necessary this year but, to add variety to an otherwise monotonous show, they decided to leave it in.

Bill Hays seemed quite relieved at the end of the Prayer when he heard no applause as he said, "You can never tell what a Republican will do."

Senator Lodge next asked the Lord to bless everybody but Wilson. I got Bill Hays on the phone and asked him, "Bill why has Lodge got it in so for Woodrow?" He said, "Well, Lodge is sore because he took Mrs. Wilson to Europe instead of him." I said, "But why didn't he pray for something terrible to happen to Bryan?" He said, "Something terrible has already happened to him."

June 10, 1920

This is not a Convention; it is a Chatauqua.

I phoned Bill Hays, "Who is praying today?" He told me, "The audience."

I said, "What do you think of the Slush Fund?" He said, "I think it is great."

I said, "How can you tell who bought delegates and who didn't?"

"Why," he said, "that's easy to tell. The fellows who haven't got any delegates haven't bought any."

June 11, 1920

I phoned Bill Hays, "Why don't some of them say something?" He said, "Well, I guess they have told all they know about Wilson."

I said, "Why surely some of all these thousands of Republicans must know of him poisoning a well or dynamiting an orphan asylum or something."

Bryan attended the Republican Convention. He wanted to see how they nominate a President.

Prohibition has raised the price of votes. Votes that used to cost a dozen 5 cent beers are now selling for a four dollar bottle of hair tonic. And the tough part of it is they are no better votes.

The Republicans nominated Senator Warren G. Harding of Ohio for its Presidential candidate and Governor Calvin Coolidge of Massachusetts for his running mate.

JUNE 14, 1920

Only two detrimental things have come out since Nomination in Harding's whole record. One was his middle name, Gamaliel, and the other he used to play a slide trombone in a country band. Musical circles in Washington are now looking towards a big revival.

Ohio claims they are due a President as they haven't had one since Taft. Look at the United States, they haven't had one since Lincoln.

My idea of an honest man is a fellow who will pay income tax on money he sold his vote for. Politicians who buy votes with Wood Alcohol will have to be very careful to not deliver the drink till after the party has voted.

Chicago crooks say it was the poorest convention on record as all the Delegates had were their badges.

* * *

JUNE 15, 1920

When I learned that President Wilson was not going to the Democratic WeeGee Convention at San Francisco I decided to go to the White House where the orders would be phoned out. The Pres. and I sat at the phones listening.

After the Chairman had finally given out, I woke President Wilson up and asked him how he liked the speech. The President said, "It was all right but he left out part of it." I said, "How do you know that?" Mr. Wilson said, "If you write anything and then rehearse a man for days just how to say it, you are pretty apt to remember if he leaves anything out."

I said, "Well, what he left out certainly was not about the Republicans as he seemed to have that part in there. The way Cummings talked it was the Republican Soldiers' fault every time the Americans had to retreat in the war. But every time we advanced it was the Democrats doing it. But, Pres, there were fewer big words in there than in most of your speeches."

He said, "Will, I had to make it plain. Did you ever see a bunch of delegates?"

JUNE 27, 1920

I asked President Wilson if he was going to listen over the phones to the speeches nominating candidates. He said, "Will, haven't I gone through enough without having to listen to them?"

I asked him, "Mr. President, are these men as great as these nominating speeches say they are?"

He said, "Will, I'll let you decide that."

I said, "Pres, I have read your Platform and I want you to explain a few things to me. Now, you all declare for freedom of speech. We must have that already or what you Politicians have said about each other, why, without it they could be put in jail.

"Soldier's compensation, I see you advocate generosity to Soldiers but also say the people shouldn't be taxed any more. Suppose the soldiers are to get together and float a loan among themselves."

I see where some of these Candidates are running out of money and are giving their Delegates IOUs.

JULY 1, 1920

I said, "Pres, there is a lot more enthusiasm in San Francisco than with the Republicans in Chicago."

Pres. said, "Yes, but that don't mean anything. A noisy vote don't count any more than a quiet one."

I said, "It's too bad you can't handle the Senate [*with which Wilson was having trouble over the League of Nations*] like you do those fellows at the Convention."

He said, "I could if it hadn't been for a lot of Republicans buying in there."

I said, "But you Democrats during the war must have made Government jobs look so good that the Republicans figured they could make money out of them even after paying a big price for them."

The Democratic WeeGee Convention nominated Governor James M. Cox of Ohio for its Presidential candidate and Assistant Secretary of the Navy, Franklin D. Roosevelt, for its Vice-Presidential victim.

JULY 4, 1920

Harding is sending out his speeches on the Phonograph. Well, us public have one consolation – a record when dropped breaks easily.

Can you imagine anything more cheerful than a party of friends gathered, opening home brew, and listening to a record, "Voters, if I am elected, I will enforce the law to the letter."

The Democrats nominated Roosevelt for Vice-President on account of his name, I suppose, figuring that most progressives were so far behind they wouldent know the difference.

Vice Presidents answer about the same purpose as a flank cinch on a saddle. If you break the front one, you are worse off than if you had no other.

The Democrats cant compete with the Republicans in spending money to get in office but after they get in I dont think there is anybody can compete with them.

Harding and Coolidge, with their slogan of a "return to normalcy" snowed Cox and Roosevelt under.

APRIL 1, 1921

Will Hays took me in to meet President Harding. I said, "Mr. President, I would like to tell you all the latest political jokes."

He said, "You don't have to, Will, I appointed them."

CHAPTER TWO

"Politics Is Applesauce"

On December 22, 1922, Will began writing his newspaper column that soon the United States began eating breakfast with. From now on he had a political forum in which to voice his viewpoints.

DECEMBER 22, 1922

I have never mixed up in Politics therefore I am able to tell the truth. So you all are going from time to time to get the real low down on some of these Birds who are elected to help misrun our Government.

The more you read and observe about this Politics thing, you got to admit that each party is worse than the other. The one thats out always looks the best.

FEBRUARY 18, 1923

Congress and Hollywood are a great deal alike in lots of respects. We make in Hollywood what we think will be two kinds of Pictures, Comedy and Drama, or sad ones. Now you take the Capitol at Washington, that's the biggest Studio in the World. We call ours Pictures when they are turned out. They call theirs Laws. It's all the same thing. We often make what we think is Drama but when it is shown it is received by the audience as Comedy. So the uncertainty is about equal both places.

The way to judge a good Comedy is by how long it will last and have people talk about it. Now Congress has turned out some that have lived for years and people are still laughing about them.

They have what they call the Lower House. That compares to what we call the Scenario Department. That's where somebody gets the idea of what he thinks will make a good Comedy or Law and they argue around and put it into shape. Then it is passed along, printed, or shot, or Photographed, as we call it, then it reaches the Senate or the Cutting and Titling Department.

Now, in our Movie Studios we have what we call Gag Men whose sole business is just to furnish some little Gag, or Amendment as they call it, which will get a laugh or perhaps change the whole thing around.

Now the Senate has what is considered the best and highest priced Gag Men that can be collected anywhere. Why, they put in so many little gags or amendments that the poor Author of the thing dont know his own story.

They consider if a man can sit there in the Studio in Washington and just put in one funny amendment in each Bill, or production, that will change it from what it originally meant, why, he is considered to have earned his pay.

Take for instance the Prohibition Production that was introduced in the Congress as a Comedy.

Well, when it come up in the Senate, one of the Gag

or Title Men (A Shepherd or Sheep Man from Texas) [*Senator Morris Sheppard*] says, "I got an Idea; instead of this just being a joke and doing away with the Saloons, why, I will put in a Title here that will say do away with everything."

So they sent around to all the Bars in Washington and got a Quorum and released what was to be a harmless little Comedy made over into a Tragedy.

Now, Folks, why patronize California-made Productions? The Capitol Comedy Co. of Washington D. C. have never had a failure. They are every one 100 percent funny or 100 percent sad.

MARCH 16, 1923

Lincoln made a wonderful speech one time: "That this nation under God shall have a new Birth of Freedom, and that Government of the People, by the People, for the People shall not perish from this earth."

Now, every time a Politician gets in a speech, he digs up this Gettysburg quotation. He recites it every Decoration day and practices the opposite 364 days. Now Lincoln meant well but he only succeeded in supplying an applause line for every Political Speaker who was stuck for a finish.

President Harding died in August, 1923, and Calvin Coolidge became President.

SEPTEMBER 16, 1923

William J. Bryan is waiting till he finds out where the next Democratic Convention will be held, and then be there ready to knock any aspiring Presidential Candidate on the head the minute it shows above the mob.

Bryan's speeches have been the only thing to look forward to at a Democratic Convention for years. He has sent more Presidential Candidates home without a Reception Committee meeting them than any Monologist living. He can take a batch of words and scramble them together and leaven them properly with a hunk of Oratory and knock the White House door knob right out of a Candidates hand.

NOVEMBER 11, 1923

If I was running I would be ashamed to let anybody know which one of those Parties I belonged to. Now, take the last three years, it looked like the Democratic Party was the best Party. But the 8 years previous to that it looked like the Republican Party was the best. The only way in the World to make either one look half decent is to keep them out.

Now you take, for instance, a Republican. There is lots of People that wont speak or associate with one. They think they would catch some grafting Disease but I have met several of them and you take one, when he is out of office, and he is as nice a fellow as you would want to meet. You keep a Republican broke and out of office and pretty near anybody can get along with them.

Now, on the other hand, take the Democrats. They are a great deal like France. France wants to so entirely crush Germany that they will never be able to rise up and attack them again. Well, that is the way with the

Democrats. Every time they got in office and started to get ahead and accumulated something, why the Republicans would rise up and crush them. They didn't even wait for 40 years like the Germans, but would generally pounce on them about every 4 years.

You take a Democrat and a Republican and you keep them both out of office and I bet you they will turn out to be good friends and maybe make useful Citizens and devote their time to some work instead of 'lectioneering all the time.

JUNE 8, 1924

A friend of mine from Texas, a member of the House, saw me sitting up in the Gallery and he called attention and introduced me to the House of Representatives. Well, I felt that quite a compliment but there was nothing I could do. An ordinary Comedian like me would have no chance there. I was the most unfunny man in the entire building.

Then I went downstairs outside the Congress Hall and I want to tell you they are as fine a bunch of men as you ever met in your life. That is when you catch them when they havent Politics on their Minds.

But the minute they get in that immense Hall they begin to get Serious and it's then that they do such Amusing things.

If we could just send the same bunch of men to Washington for the good of the Nation, and not for Political Reasons, we could have the most perfect Government in the World.

JUNE 10, 1924

After all, this running for President is sort of a hazardous business. Statistics have proven that out of 110 million people there is only one gets to be President. It's what you might call a Long Shot office, and you can't condemn a Man for not investing in Campaign Literature.

CHAPTER THREE

Cal Coolidge Had Them Cold

The 1924 Republican Convention held in Cleveland was the first that Will ever attended in person.

JUNE 8, 1924

As I pen these lines I am waiting for my train to carry me to the Coolidge Follies in Cleveland. At first I was going to say the Republican Follies but it's not. They have nothing to do with it. The whole thing is under the personal supervision of Mr. Coolidge.

Now can you imagine Yaps like us going to Cleveland from all over the country when Mr. Coolidge is not going to be there himself? It's like going to see Sir Harry Lauder's show without Sir Harry.

Coolidge could have been nominated by post card. Those misled Delegates will have just as much chance to really nominate him as a Bow Legged girl would have at our Stage Door [*the Follies*].

All my life I have been longing to attend a convention and now I draw this one. My disappointment is just like a sick man who has been promised a trip to a circus for years. Then when he is able to go out they take him to Grant's Tomb.

You can tell a New England delegate. He will be eating a box lunch which he brought from home in the hotel lobby.

JUNE 10, 1920

The Republican Vice-President conscription convention opened at 11 o'clock with an array of badges that was deafening.

I had the thrill of my life. I entered the convention press stand with William Jennings Bryan. We were the only two aliens in the entire hall – he the solitary Democrat and I the sole remaining Progressive Bull Moose.

As we walked over from the hotel everybody recognized Bryan and spoke. Finally a traffic policeman recognized me and said, "I saw one of your movies last night; they flatter you."

Bryan and I sat together in the press stand. Everybody thought I was a plainclothes man sent along to protect Bryan from the Republicans.

As we entered the hall everybody stood up. Both of us looked at each other rather embarrassed, as we dident know which one the demonstration was meant for. But we found they were rising to sing one of our national anthems which, by the way, the Republicans dont know any better than the plain people.

It will take America two more wars to learn the words of our national hymn.

Bryan said to me, "You write a humorous column, don't you?"

I looked around to see if anybody was listening and then I said, "Yes, sir."

He said, "Well, I write a serious article and if I think of anything of a comical or funny nature, I will give it to you."

I thanked him and told him, "If I happen to think of anything of a serious nature, I will give it to you."

When he said he wrote seriously and I said I wrote humorously, I thought afterward we both may be wrong.

JUNE 11, 1924

I dont want to appear disrespectful, or lacking in devotion to prayer, but when prayer has been the outstanding feature of both days I cant help but record the fact. They are getting longer each day. I dont know if that is through necessity or not. This one today was a keynote prayer.

It was the only strictly political oration I ever heard delivered in the guise of prayer. I had never heard prayer have a text like sermons. His was "Republican Party Unity." The only reference to anything pertaining to the Bible was the word "Amen" at the finish.

He was by far the best orator that has appeared.

Mr. Bryan and I are the Weber and Fields of the convention. You remember one of them used to get just as many laughs as the other.

So today I am taking the serious side of the convention and he is taking the comedy. Of course he assists me with serious suggestions, for instance, here is one he told me today:

"Senator Lodge passed by a little girl and her mother up in Massachusetts, and the little girl said, 'Oh, mamma, ain't Mr. Lodge the meanest man in the world?' and the mother scolded the child very sharply and said, 'How often have I told you not to use the word ain't!' "

A lady was the best thing on the program today. She was to introduce Mr. Mondell of Wyoming as the Chairman of the convention. She simply walked down front and said, "Convention, I submit to you Mr. Mondell."

If that had been some politician introducing him, they would have had to drag in the glory of every past Republican President as far back as Lincoln, and it would have taken an hour for him to have thought of them all.

What she left out he immediately said. He said, "This Chairmanship is the greatest honor that can come to any man." Now he knows that is a lot of applesauce, for a Chairman at one of those conventions is nothing more than an auctioneer with a hammer receiving and taking the delegates' yeses and noes.

June 13, 1924

I love Cleveland because I knew them before this catastrophe struck them. She will arise from her badges and some day be greater than ever. But I had to leave. I simply couldn't stand the incessant din, the roar, the popping of corks, and the newness and brightness of the speeches, and the "fairness to other political parties" uttered from the platform. I just had to have a rest and return to the solitude and quiet of a Ziegfeld rehearsal where everything is still and orderly as a prayer meeting.

P.S. Before they forget it, why, they nominated Coolidge.

It has been rumored around town today that I left to prevent my being nominated as Vice President. I wish to state that that was exactly the case.

Well, so long, readers — both of you. Will meet you at the Democratic convention again. What it lacks in class, why, they will make up in noise.

Tip to prospective delegates who are coming: Leave your watches and jewelry at home. Bring nothing but your alternates. It's a cinch you can't lose them.

The Republicans had trouble selecting a Vice-Presidential candidate. Half a dozen times a man was picked, Coolidge was called to ask if the man was satisfactory, and his invariable answer was "yes." Finally Charles (Hell-and-Marie) Dawes was nominated.

Later, Will asked Coolidge why he did not help select his own running mate.

"Nobody told them in 1920 and they did all right," Coolidge said.

CHAPTER FOUR

The 1924 Democratic "Follies"

The Democratic National Convention in 1924 was not only the longest political convention in history but also one of the most bitterly fought. Not since the Civil War, when the party went to pieces over the slavery question, had there been so much recrimination.

The party of Woodrow Wilson was split wide open by the Ku Klux Klan question, prohibition, a widening breach between the West and the South, and the East, and diverse religious and personal questions.

Two figures — poles apart — dominated the scene: William Gibbs McAdoo, prohibitionists, and Al Smith, outspoken wet and about the only member of the party in the east and north who was "working." He sort of had the governorship of the State of New York in his vest pocket. Oddly enough, although a Tammany man, he was a staunch liberal and of unquestioned honesty.

JUNE 22, 1924

Sunday morning, at the depot at Atlantic City, two special trains were standing side by side. One was our train carrying the Ziegfeld Follies Company back to New

York after a week's tryout of the new show. The other was for a bunch of Delegates going to the Democratic Convention in New York. Nobody seemed to know which to take, so, being an accommodating kind of person, I called out:

"On your left for the Ziegfeld Follies show and on your right for *the Democratic Consolation Show.*"

Now both shows open Tuesday. The Democrats go to Madison Square Garden, where Ringling Brothers' Circus always plays, and we go to the Amsterdam Theatre, a beautiful theatre consecrated solely to Art.

We think we have the best show we have ever had. They think they have the best show they ever had.

It's the first time in the theatrical history of New York City where two shows of equal magnitude both open on the same night.

It means "Man versus Women." They are featuring Men, and we are featuring Women.

I don't mean to appear partisan, just because I am with the Woman Show, but I think Women will outdraw Men as an attraction every time.

Can you imagine any one going into a big barn of a place to see Al Smith, when they can go into a comfortable Theatre and see 100 of the most beautiful Creatures on earth? I tell you it's not in the cards.

Now, take Bill McAdoo; he is a dandy, nice fellow, and I like him personally, but do you think I would go into a place to look at him when I could see Ann Pennington's knees?

Of course, they may get a few of the riff raff, because some people will go to see anything.

But the class won't be there. They have got to get the class in their show to draw them in. Why, we have Imogene Wilson in our show, and she is better known than all their candidates put together.

And the costuming: to compare that is a joke! Can you imagine my old friend William J. Bryan's old alpaca coat stacked up against the creations Evelyn Law and Martha Lauber will have on?

Mind you, I am not criticizing any man's grooming (in fact, I couldn't). But when you come into New York to open, you naturally have to compete with what New York rival attractions have to offer.

Now these politicians' suits are all right in the Chautauquas (they know they are, for they have tried them for years), but not for New York.

The only thing they have on us is the badges. We are simply outbadged. Now, if you just want to look at badges and no beauty, why there is where you want to go, for as a badge display it is a total success.

Of course, we could put badges on our girls, but who wants to see a Follies' girl overdressed.

June 22, 1924

The city is doing all it can to make their stay here remembered. The Mayor issued orders that no delegate was to be robbed until after the convention was called to order.

It was a beautiful Sunday here. The New York churches

were crowded with New Yorkers. Coney Island was crowded with delegates.

It may have been a coincidence, but every preacher in town preached on "Honesty in Government."

JUNE 23, 1924

The Democrats can adjourn right now (which is 6 o'clock on the evening before it's billed to start) and they will have been a better convention than the Republicans had.

In fact, I suggested to them that if I was them I would adjourn before they nominated somebody and spoiled it all.

Excitement? Why, there are more bands playing in this town than there were delegates at Cleveland.

A State that didn't send at least two bands had their Badges taken away from them.

If they had had that many bands and delegations parading all in different directions out in Cleveland, why they would have had to borrow some streets from Toledo or Youngstown.

Al Smith copped off Fifth Avenue for his parade, and it took five hours for his followers to stagger by a given point.

Mr. McAdoo phoned me to come over to the Vanderbilt Hotel at 9:30 to meet the California delegation. They arrived about noon. We found out the Los Angeles delegation had been selling lots to customers all along the line of march.

Mr. McAdoo came out on the balcony of the hotel and

made a very good speech, while the delegates went through the crowd and took first payments on choice corner lots in Hollywood.

JUNE 25, 1924

Well, the Democratic scandals got started yesterday. The thing was almost an hour late in starting. You could tell the delegates who had been entertained by Tammy men the night before. They looked awful, and must have felt terrible.

The building is literally lined with flags. I could never understand the exact connection between the flag and a bunch of politicians. Why a political speaker's platform should be draped in flags any more than a factory where men work, or an office building, is beyond me.

A man handed around in the press stands some thick paperback books. I asked, "Is this the life of Old Hickory?" He said, "No, that is Pat Harrison's keynote speech." He told things on the Republicans that would have made anybody but Republicans ashamed of themselves.

When he mentioned old Andy Jackson, he just knocked those Democrats off their seats. Then, as he saw they were recovering, he hit 'em with the name of Thomas Jefferson, and that rocked them back. Then he mentioned Woodrow Wilson, and that sent them daffy.

I am not up on political etiquette, but it struck me as rather strange, after paying a tribute to a wonderful man, that the delegates should raise up and start shouting and singing "Hail, Hail, the Gang's All Here, What the Hell Do We Care." They hollered and shouted and sang "John

Brown's Body" and "Tipperary." Even my old Side-Kick Bryan, was prancing around the hall shouting.

Now, he has been brought up different. He has read the Bible, even if it was just to get quotations from, but he knows, even if those other delegates didn't, that that was no way to pay tribute to a martyred President.

As poor as the Republican Convention was I will give them credit, they didn't sing "Hail, Hail, the Gang's All Here" when the speaker mentioned Lincoln.

The whole thing looked like a sure stampede for Wilson. So there will be a terrible disappointment when the delegates find that he has passed beyond and won't be able to accept.

Chairman Cordell Hull read what the convention was gathered here for: "That it was to nominate a man to run for President and take any other drastic means necessary."

Mayor Hylan made a welcoming speech to the convention. It was on "Honesty in Private and Government Affairs." I don't see why he should lecture the delegates. They are not going to get away with anything in this town.

But he did have a sure fire finish to his act. He said, "I have told them to issue you little cards that will be good for every so-called private place in New York."

June 26, 1924

The following is one of the bravest statements made in a political decade:

In the entire three years of preparation by the Democratic Party to groom some man for this present crisis there has never been a mention of a man to run for Vice President.

You see every man that wants to run at all wants to be President and a man would take his life in his hands to go and ask one of those fellows if he was willing to run for second place. It's bad enough to be nominated for President much less Vice President on that ticket.

So I just got off and held a caucus with myself and said somebody has got to be sacrificed for the sake of party harmony. I hereby and hereon put myself in nomination, and to save some other man being humiliated by having to put me in nomination, why, I will just nominate myself.

So, I, Will Rogers, of Claremore, Okla.; Hollywood, Cal., and 42nd St. and Broadway, New York, do hereby step right out and declare myself, not only as a receptive but an anxious candidate for the husband's position (meaning second) on the forthcoming Democratic ticket.

On first hearing this it may sound like a joke, but when I relate to you come of the qualifications which I possess, why, I think any fair-minded man will give me serious consideration.

In the first place, they have got to nominate a farmer who understands the farmers' condition. Well, I got two farms in Oklahoma, both mortgaged, so no man knows their condition better than I do.

He has also to be a man from the West. Well, if a man came from 25 feet further West than I lived last year, he would have to be a fish in the Pacific Ocean.

Dawes was nominated on the Republican ticket on account of his profanity. Now I have never tried cussin' in public, but I guess I could learn to get used to it before a crowd.

Another big reason why I should be nominated is I am not a Democrat. Another still bigger reason why I should be nominated is I am not a Republican. I am just progressive enough to suit the dissatisfied. And lazy enough to be a Stand Patter.

Oil has never touched me. The reason I know it never has is, I drilled a well on my farm in Oklahoma, and I never even touched it, much less oil touching me.

I never worked for a big corporation.

When the President can't go anywhere, why, the Vice President has to go and speak or eat for him. Now, I could take in all the dinners, for I am a fair eater.

I could say, "I am sorry the President can't come, but he had pressing business." Of course, I wouldn't tell the real reason why he didn't come, so I am just good enough a liar to be a good Vice President.

I am not much of an after-dinner speaker, but I could learn two stories, one for dinners where ladies were present, and one for where they were not.

Of course I have no dress suit. The Government would have to furnish me a dress suit. If I went to a dinner in a rented one, they would mistake me for a Congressman.

I know I can hear a lot of you all say, "Yes, Will, you would make a good Vice President, but suppose something happened to the President?"

Well, I would do just like Mr. Coolidge — I would go in there and keep still and say nothing. He is the first

President to discover that what the American people want is to be let alone.

It won't take much to launch the boom. We will wait till about tomorrow, and when some dark or even light horse is eliminated, we can take their headquarters, and buy their buttons and badges cheap.

P.S. I was born in a Log Cabin.

JUNE 27, 1924

We have heard nothing since 10 o'clock this morning until 6 tonight but "The man I am going to name." Then they talk for another thirty minutes and then, "The man I am going to name." There have been guys going to name men all day, and all we ever got named were about six out of a possible 200.

Franklin Roosevelt started in early this morning with the "Man I am about to name." He had the opportunity of a lifetime to make a name for himself comparable with the Republican end of the Roosevelt family. But no, he must say, "Man I am about to name" for ten pages.

But when he did get to the end and named Al Smith you would have thought somebody had thrown a wildcat in your face. The galleries went wild and about ten State delegations marched and hollered for an hour. Talk about our civilization! Why, if they ever took a sanity test at a political convention 98 per cent. would be removed to an asylum.

Oh, yes, a woman from Oregon seconded McAdoo for the ninth time. She didn't have to come. She could have stood on the banks of the Columbia River in Oregon and we could have heard her perfectly. I bet she busted every radio east of the Mississippi.

Talk about Presidential Timber, why, Man, they had whole Lumber Yards of it here. There was so many being Nominated that some of the men making the nominating Speeches had never even met the men they were nominating. I know they had not from the way they talked about them.

A guy from Utah talked so long and loud that all of us couldn't see how it could be anybody in the world he was nominating but Brigham Young – "that matchless father" – but he crossed everybody by seconding McAdoo's nomination.

JUNE 28, 1924

I saw something yesterday that for stupidity, lack of judgment, nonsensicality, unexcitement, uselessness and childishness, has anything I've ever seen beaten. It was the Democratic Convention.

These delegates are like prisoners in a way. They have got to listen to everyone who gets up there and takes up their time is simply hitting a man when he is down. Not only doing that, but robbing him.

Can you imagine a theatre audience sitting there listening to the same old hokum over and over again? Why, they would get the hook in you so fast these delegates would be back home in three days.

There is a society in this town that stops us when we abuse or unnecessarily annoy a bucking horse or wild steer right in this same Madison Square Garden. Now why in the world don't they get busy and protect a delegate?

Now I never propose a thing unless I have a solution to it. Make every speaker, as soon as he tells all he knows, sit down. That will shorten your speeches so much you will be out by lunch time every day.

Or make them be censored and not allow one man to repeat what some other man had already said. That would cut it down to just one speech at each convention.

Now, I hope you will pardon me for not being funny. But I like these delegates, and I want to try and do them a service that they will thank me for as long as they live.

JULY 4, 1920

This thing has got to come to an end. These delegates and visitors may not know it but right where they are sitting and sleeping every day is New York's municipal swimming hole. Summer is on us here and you visitors are depriving New York of their annual bath.

New York invited you people here as guests, not to live.

One delegation told me yesterday that they either had to move to more modest quarters or to a more liberal candidate.

The tough part of it is that it is not like the convention you read about in the papers sixty-four years ago that had to move from Charleston to Baltimore. They can't move this one. No other town will take it.

A second-hand convention is one of the hardest things to get rid of in the world.

The thing has just got to break pretty soon as the women delegates' badges are wearing holes through their shirt waists and the convention will turn into an exposure in two more days.

Another reason I know it can't last much longer is that the women who sit in front, on the speakers' platform, are about to run out of different hats to wear. They would rather lose the election than wear the same hat twice.

JULY 5, 1924

The biggest celebration ever held in honor of a President's birthday was held in Madison Square Garden yesterday in honor of the fifty-second birthday of Calvin Coolidge.

Met at 1 o'clock and my friend, Mr. Augustus Thomas, the orator and playwright, read what was called the Declaration of Independence. Nobody knows how they ever found a copy of it. The J. P. Morgan private library has most all those old things, so I guess he loaned it to them.

The delegates seemed mildly amused as he read this strange old legend.

On its completion a delegate at large from Georgia offered an amendment to the Declaration of Independence which the Chairman read. Ohio called for a poll of their delegation in case the Declaration came to a vote.

Mr. Thomas explained before starting to read it that it was written by Thomas Jefferson, a Democrat. Had its author happened to have been a Republican it would have been denounced as a Senatorial Oligarchy.

Bryan didn't speak today. I'll bet you that this is the first Fourth of July in fifty years he did not lecture to the fortunate dead at Arlington or somewhere else.

JULY 6, 1924

Two delegates from Arizona, each with one-half vote, cast their one vote for Will Rogers for President. In his dressing room at the New Amsterdam Theater Will gave an interview to the New York Times *reporter.*

I cannot talk statesmanship clothed in the habiliments of the art of Thespis. I must change from my stage costume.

Will put on his necktie.

This is a very serious moment in the destinies of the nation. The Democratic Party is locked in a stranglehold and can make no progress. My candidacy represents nothing more than the effort of the plain people — of which I am one — to remedy this disastrous condition of affairs.

It is my duty to go directly to the scene of the conflict and marshal the forces of right and justice. I do not seek this office, but respond to public demand in the spirit in which Spartacus left his plow in the furrow. I leave my Ford in the ditch and go to lead the movement to which the unanimous vote of that lone Arizona delegate — who deserves a high place in the country's roll of patriots — calls.

The hour demands a leader. The voice of the people calls. Who am I that I should hesitate?

My plan of campaign is to go along until all the other

candidates have begun to show signs of weakening about Labor Day, and then throw in my reserve.

We shall make a brief whirlwind campaign. That is the way we have started. I have already explained how my vote has practically doubled without me turning a hand, and when we throw in the reserve, that will make three of us. And believe me, we will be as obstinate as the rest of them.

What I will have to do first thing is to get a good campaign manager. You might announce that any retired business man looking for a safe place to invest about $25,000 with a partnership in the concern, references exchanged, will be welcome in this capacity. His work will be very light. I'd figure he wouldn't have any more to do than sign the check. I'll take all the labor of spending it off his hands.

And I'd like to have the word passed around quietly that I can be bought. But let them know, to save time, that I don't intend to sell out the delegate who has flocked to my support cheap. I'm not naming any figure, but my Rolls Royce needs a new tire on the left hind foot.

JULY 7, 1924

The Democratic Convention adjourned and held another miniature one with only the managers of the candidates there, which meant, perhaps some seventy or eighty men.

Mr. Bryan and I write for the same syndicate, and we meet every evening around 6 in their office writing and filing our stories. We always have a friendly chat (as I don't think he reads my articles; only reads his own).

He said that he was going to this conference of candidates' managers. I said, "How is that?" He said, "Why, I am my brother's manager." I said, "Why, your brother only has two votes; so that you won't feel lonesome up there with those two, why, you can also represent me with my one."

I got afraid after that he would sell me out. But no, what do you think he did? He goes up there in this important conference and goes sound asleep.

Can you beat my luck picking out a campaign manager to represent me like that? I felt terrible about it at first, but when I got to thinking of what the other members of the conference gained by his going to sleep, I figured that I could sacrifice my interests just to have them enjoy a few minutes peace. With him asleep I bet you it was the most successful one he ever attended.

I have been asked repeatedly if I was going to withdraw. No, sir, I am not. Why should I show myself as being the only gentleman in the race by withdrawing.

JULY 9, 1924

Well, it was 6:30 and they had just read the platform. I had it before me, forty-five pages. If it had come out in the open on every question and told just where they stood, they could have saved themselves, not only forty-two pages of paper, but perhaps their election in November.

When you straddle a thing it takes a long time to explain it.

It favors fixing everything the Republicans have ruined, keeping everything that they haven't, right up to its present standard. In the Republican platform at Cleveland they promised to do better.

I don't think they have done so bad this time. Everybody's broke but them.

JULY 10, 1924

Who said miracles don't happen? Didn't the Democratic National Convention nominate a man at last?

That should bring more people back to religion than any other one thing. It has been a demonstration of faith, because, after all, God is good.

This convention wound up in a personal triumph for William Jennings Bryan. My old friend W. J. is the greatest character we have in this country today. He is a very unique man. Most of us only attract attention twice on earth. One is when we are born and the other is when we die.

But Mr. Bryan even improves on a bear; a bear hibernates all Winter, but Bryan hibernates for four years, and then emerges, and has a celebration every four years at every Democratic Convention.

In the meantime, he lectures in tents, shooting galleries, grain elevators, snow sheds or any place that he can find a bunch of people that haven't got a radio.

No one has ever been able to understand the unique and uncanny power that he seems to hold over the Democratic Party, especially near nominating time. Since 1896 he has either run himself or named the man that would run.

And then all during the convention here you would hear the expression, "Well, poor old man Bryan! He has lost his grip on the delegates. Here is one where he won't be able to name the man." But not me; I never wavered.

When he came out *against* Davis, Davis was a nominated man. Those eleven hundred delegates said, "If Bryan is so set against him he must be the right man."

Next to Bryan the New York papers have killed off more deserving candidates by supporting them.

CHAPTER FIVE

The Great Big Normal Majority

August 24, 1924

I was just reading all day yesterday and today President Coolidge's Serial on the Republican Administration. He certainly has been saving up. The question arises whether a man who has been an established success and gained the confidence of the American people by not shooting off on everything that comes up — whether it is good Policy for him to break that rule. Personally I think he made a mistake.

I don't care how smart you are, if you say something you are liable to say something foolish, and the smarter you are, and the longer you talk the more Fool things you will say. We had pictured him as the quiet active man that Does instead of Says. But No, like all Republicans, he has been badly advised and now he is just a Politician seeking re-election.

October 19, 1924

I have been trying to read the papers and see just what it is in this election that one Party wants that the other one don't. To save my soul I can't find any difference. The only thing that I can see where they differ is that the Democrats want the Republicans to get out and let them in, and the Republicans don't want to get out.

They are so hard up for an issue that Mr. Coolidge has finally just announced his policy will be Common Sense. Well, don't you know the Democrats will claim that too? Do you think they will call their campaign "Darn Foolishness"?

Besides, Common Sense is not an Issue in Politics; it's an affliction.

Davis announced that his Policy will be Honesty. Neither is that an issue in Politics; it's a Miracle, and can he get enough people that believes in Miracles to elect him?

The only thing I see now that the two old line Parties are divided on is the question, "Who will have the Post Offices?"

OCTOBER 26, 1924

The Literary Digest should change its name to the Literary Poll Test because it is impossible for the Weather Department to announce rain on a certain day without the digest taking a Straw Vote on the matter.

They got one Poll running now on, "Who do you guess will be President?"

It's the only publication that don't already know who will be.

Coolidge is away ahead and all the Republican Papers are saying that it is absolutely the fairest way to get the real sentiment of the entire Country.

The Democratic Papers claim that the whole thing is a fiend of Purgatory, and a tool of the interests.

Personally I don't think this straw vote demonstrates but one thing: that is that there are more Republicans that can write than there are Democrats. Now when it comes to voting, a Man can make a cross and get somebody to write his name. But on these cards he don't know what he might be signing away. A Democrat hasn't got much left as it is and he don't want to take any chances on losing what little he has.

More men have been elected by Straw Votes to office, and fewer received Salary, than any other industry in America.

The same men that straw vote are the ones who can sit down all day and play Solitaire. It's like winning on the races in your mind. No mathematician in this country has ever been able to figure out how many hundred straw votes it takes to equal one legitimate vote.

NOVEMBER 3, 1924

I would wait and write this after election, but the fellow who don't know how this election is going to come out, even a month before it happened, he should not be allowed to read a Paper and probably can't.

Of course some of the County Offices, and Sheriffs and road Commissioners may be in doubt up to the counting time.

I hope some of the men who get the most votes will be elected. That is of course not generally the case. If I was running for office I would rather have two friends in the counting room than a Republican Slush fund behind me. More candidates have been defeated after 6 oclock in the evening than were ever defeated during election day.

Some Guy at this Senatorial investigation said that he could have bought for 50 thousand dollars jokes on the stage in favor of any certain Candidate. Gosh, I wish I had known that! I would have been rich by now! If I had collected for every favorable joke I have told about each one of the Candidates, and if I had been paid for all I had told against each one of them I would be a Millionaire. I have said something good about them when they have done something good, and I have knocked them when they didn't do no good. That is why I am generally knocking them.

I generally give the Party in Power, whether Republican or Democratic, the more digs because they are generally doing the Country the most damage, and besides I don't think it is fair to jump too much on the fellow who is down. He is not working, he is only living in hopes of getting back in on the graft in another four years, while the Party in power is drawing a Salary to be knocked.

November 16, 1924

Well, the election is finally over. The result was just as big a surprise as the announcement that Christmas was coming in December.

The Republicans mopped up, the Democrats gummed up, and I will now try and sum up.

This next Congress will be composed partly of men who were defeated in the late Democratic annihilation.

That is, it will be composed of what is known as Lame Ducks. There is no other business in the world that allows a man to work after he is fired except politics. Politics is different from any other business; in fact it is different from anything. So, plainly speaking, a Lame Duck is a politician who has had his salary shot from under him.

Now let us sum up and see just how Mr. Coolidge polled this big majority.

I personally lay some of it to the congested traffic. On election day the Republican Chauffers in their Pierce Arrows crowded the poor Democrats out so they couldn't get to the Polls in their Fords.

But the big reason I told Mr. and Mrs. Alice Nicholas Longworth last June after returning from California and also visiting various states coming back East. They asked me, "Will, how does Coolidge stand all over the country?" I told them, "He is very very strong. He has a kind of uncanny hold of the people. They all seem to be for giving him a chance. They know he had nothing personally to do with all this oil mess, and he inherited a lot of ills for which he was not to blame." It's just an illustration of the fairness of the great mass of people, or crowd fairness.

If you went to any sporting event and one of the principals in it was unable to go on and they substituted another for his part you would see the big majority of that crowd with the substitute.

Now that we have summed up on how and why he won, let us sum up on why the Democrats lost.

You can't beat an Administration by attacking it. You have to show some plan on improving it.

Now you got 4 years to think of something original. Mr. Coolidge thought of the idea of keeping still. Too bad you all didn't think of that. But you didn't, and he did so give him credit.

Now if you can't think of anything by next election I would just give up your Democratic Franchise and join the Republicans. This criticism is offered by an unbiased Sportsman who just loves to see a close race.

FEBRUARY 22, 1925

No Element, no Party, not even Congress or the Senate can hurt this Country now; it's too big. That's why I can never take a Politician seriously.

Nobody is making History. Everybody is just drifting along with the tide. If any office holder feels he is carrying a burden of responsibility, some Fly will light on his back and scratch it off for him some day. Congress can pass a bad law and as soon as the old Normal Majority find it out they have it scratched off the books.

Even when our next War comes we will through our shortsightedness not be prepared, but that won't be anything fatal. The real energy and minds of the Normal Majority will step in and handle it and fight it through to a successful conclusion.

It's just the same as it was, and always will be, because it is founded on right and even if everybody in Public Life tried to ruin it they couldn't.

This Country is not where it is today on account of any man. It is here on account of the real common Sense of the big Normal Majority.

CHAPTER SIX

Between Follies, 1925–1928

MARCH 7, 1925

Well, all the papers have been full of the Inauguration, commenting on the simplicity of it, some of them for and some others against. I don't think you can stir up a whole lot of excitement over a Man getting up out of his seat, and sitting down in the same seat again.

Now if it had been somebody else, say for instance that sterling Statesman, and fearless Leader, YOURS TRULY! had won out, then can you imagine the excitement over the Inauguration?

I would have showed you some life. Instead of having a delegation of those side hill Farmers from Vermont (with one leg longer than the other, from following a walking Plow around those steep hills) here is an Illustration of just a few of the Delegations that I would have had there:

In the first place I would have had every Cherokee Indian of my Tribe there. Then I would have had a bunch of my Cowboy friends there. (That has not been done since Teddy Roosevelt was inaugurated.) I would have used them to rope and drag the Lobbyists in Washington up Pennsylvania Avenue in the Big Parade.

Now Coolidge had a few Soldiers marching in this small time Parade. I would have had millions because I wrote Articles for the Bonus, while he vetoed it. If course, I would have been hissed by the Rich men who were not in favor of it, but what do we care, I am catering to the big majority.

Now think of the Moving Picture Delegation that I would have there. As an opening ceremony I would have Doug Fairbanks jump off the Washington Monument. He would light, and carry Mary Pickford out of the crowd on his Shoulders.

In my Movie Contingent I would have Cecil De Mille part the waters of the Potomac and let the people west of the river come over. If he divided the Dead Sea, it ought to be a cinch to handle the Potomac (it's more a name than a river anyway.)

Charlie Chaplin I would have do some funny stuff on the Capitol steps while I was delivering my Inaugural address. There has never been a President that had the foresight to think of having something done, so the people can look at it while the inaugural address is being delivered. And while they were swearing in the Vice President, Harold Lloyd could be climbing up the outside of the Lincoln Memorial.

They had a lot of Governors of different States who marched according to when they entered the Union. In place of them I would have had Ziegfeld Follies. Can you imagine anyone looking at a Governor when he could look at a Follies Girl? They would make a sucker out of those Governors.

They say they haven't had a Man that rode a Horse to the White House since Jefferson. Say, I would have been straddle of an old Buzzard head. Instead of the Marine Band, or the Government Band, Boy, I would have had Paul Whiteman's Band and George Olson's Follies band. They would have just ruined that District of Columbia air around there with White House Blues.

As my personal escort instead of a lot of plain Clothes Police, I would have had Ben Turpin. Nobody would throw a thing at me. He could be watching every way at once. Instead of Major General Hines and his Staff, I would have had Ann Pennington, Gloria Swanson, Pola Negri, Peggy Joyce and Baby Peggy.

So if Washington wants to wail about what a tame affair their Inauguration was why don't blame me. I would have showed them an Inauguration staged by Ziegfeld and D. W. Griffith that would have made them forget Vermont belonged to the Union.

March 7, 1925

Speaking of Congress, the name of Ye Editor of Ye Weekly Illiterate Digest was dragged into a discussion that happened on the floor recently. We had had the misfortune to have parts of at least 5 separate Articles read into the Yearly Joke Book (The Congressional Record) beginning with a Bonus Article I wrote a year or so ago, and lately some on Airships and Battleships, and lack of preparedness. So, when a Gentleman quoted me on the floor the other day, another member took exception and said he objected to the remarks of a Professional Joke Maker going into the Congressional Record.

Now can you beat that for jealousy among people in the same line? Calling me a Professional Joke Maker! He is right about everything but the Professional. THEY are the Professional Joke Makers. Read some of the Bills that they have passed, if you think they ain't Joke makers. I could study all my life and not think up half the amount of funny things they can think of in one Session of Congress. Besides, my jokes don't do anybody any harm. You don't have to pay any attention to them. But everyone of the Jokes those Birds make is a LAW and hurts somebody (generally everybody).

"Joke Maker!" He couldn't have coined a better term for Congress if he had been inspired. But I object to being called a Professional. I am an Amateur beside them. If I had that Guy's unconscious Humor, Ziegfeld couldn't afford to pay me I would be so funny.

Of course I can understand what he was objecting to was any common sense creeping into the Record. It was such a Novelty, I guess it did sound funny.

And, by the way, I have engaged counsel and if they ever put any more of my material in that "Record of Inefficiency" I will start suit for deformation of Character. I don't want my stuff buried where Nobody ever reads it.

MORGANTOWN, W. VA., APRIL 21, 1927

This is the home State of John W. Davis, the last Democratic sacrifice on the altar of "no policy to run on."

Notice to Democrats – Get a policy and stick to it, even if it's wrong.

April 25, 1927

Can you imagine? This town of Cleveland wants the Republican and Democratic conventions both in 1928.

A town that don't know any more than that is liable to ask for a sesquicentennial. The Republican convention will be held further West, for that's the way they are going to relieve the farmers – to let 'em see a convention. And as for the Democratic one, a sanity test will follow any town purposely asking for it.

Washington, D. C., August 31, 1927

Just finished taking scenes here in Washington for a movie of the old stage play of Hoyt's, A Texas Steer. It was the story of a man elected to Washington on bought votes. We are bringing it up to date by not changing it at all. In the stage version he didn't know what to do when he got in Congress. That part is allowed to remain as it was. He used to play poker more than Legislate. That's left in. There was a little drinking among the members at that time. For correct detail in our modern version that has been allowed to remain in.

Yours for Government
buy the people.

October, 1927

Will in an article in the Saturday Evening Post *advised Al Smith to write all Democratic organizations as follows:*

"I, Al Smith, of my own free will and accord, do this day relinquish any claim or promise that I might have of any support or Deligates at the next Democratic Convention. I don't want to hinder what little harmony there is left in the party.

I not only do not choose to run, but I refuse to run. But will give all my time and talents to work faithfully for whoever is nominated by the party."

Now, Al, if you will send 'em this letter you will look like you are sacrificing yourself, and in '32 they will nominate you by radio; they can't help it, and you will have a united Party.

A half-wit knew you all couldn't win in '24. Well, it's the same this year; you couldn't put on a revival of Thomas Jefferson and get away with it.

Al, don't let those New Yorkers kid you. You got no Platform, you got no Issue, you can't ask people to throw somebody out just because somebody else wants in. You meet too many Democratic Leaders – that's what's the matter with the Party – these same leaders not knowing any more about Public Opinion than they do. That's why they are Democratic Leaders.

Then, you New Yorkers got a wrong prospectus of things. The outsiders don't care nothing about New York, and if you think Tammany Hall is an asset, you just run and try to carry them with you and you will find you have been overhandicapped.

Now it ain't that you ain't strong, Al; you are strong – you are strong – you are the strongest thing the Democrats have had in years. No Democrat could come near you. But it's not a Democrat that you meet in the finals; it's a Republican.

Everybody is always asking, "What's the matter with the Democratic Party?" There ain't nothing wrong with it; it's a Dandy Old Party. The only thing wrong with it is the law killed it. It won't let a man vote but once, and there just ain't enough voters at one vote each to get it anywhere.

You can't lick this Prosperity thing; even the fellow that hasn't got any is all excited over the idea.

You Politicians have got to look further ahead; you always got a Putter in your hands when you ought to have a Driver.

Now, Al, I am trying to tell you how to be President, not how to be a Candidate.

JANUARY 12, 1928

As usual, the Democrats fooled everybody, including themselves, and Houston got the convention. I certainly did what I was sent here to do; I kept it out of Oklahoma.

Save me a corner room at the Rice Hotel with plenty of windows, an electric fan and mosquito netting.

JANUARY 15, 1928

Al, it just looks like I can't find anybody to write to but you and Cal. Neither one of you ever answer me, but I just don't seem to get discouraged. I just keep on writing.

A good while ago I wrote you advising you to lay off the big race till 1932, when you would have a cinch instead of a race. I have learned that you must never advise a man in Politics to do anything but run. If you advise him not too, you just lose his friendship. So its always best to advise him the way he wants to be advised.

So from now on I am advising EVERYBODY to run. In that way I will be friends with the world.

February 2, 1928

There was a piece in the paper this morning where somebody back home was seriously proposing me for President. Now when that was done as a joke it was alright, but when it's done seriously it's just pathetic. We are used to having everything named as Presidential candidates, but the country hasn't quite got to the professional comedian stage.

There is no inducement that would make me foolish enough to run for any political office. I want to be on the outside where I can be friends and joke about all of them, even the President. As long as it is all right with him, why my conscience is clear. So I hereby issue my statement which is as follows:

I don't contemplate becoming involved in a political conflict of any nature during the Autumn of 1928.

P.S. Should the Democrats, however, become successful I would accept the postoffice in Beverly Hills and Claremore, Oklahoma. I can take care of both letters.

February 24, 1928

Say, that Hoover is turning out to be a better politician than everybody gave him credit for. He is the only man since prohibition has been in that is for the drys, but not against the wets.

MARCH 4, 1928

Herbert Hoover was the food dictator during World War I. As such he spent a lot of his time in Europe.

Then when he came back why they wanted to run him for President. But it was the Democrats that wanted to run him. Well, he had been away a long time and had been out of touch with political affairs, but he hadn't been so much out of touch with them that he didn't know about what the strength of a Democratic candidate would be in 1920.

Well, the Republicans got in, and President Harding wanted to add enough respectable members to his cabinet to make it kinder balance, so he had to draft Hoover.

Well, he dragged along in the cabinet there. There is mighty little nourishment belonging to a thing like that. It's about like playing in the line in a football game. Unless you get the ball to run with, you are there to do nothing but get run over, or try to make a hole for the "headman" to come through.

When the 1924 handicap come on they offered the Vice Presidency to Mr. Hoover. Well, that was just verging on an insult, especially when you knew the good care Mr. Coolidge took of himself. So he turned it down.

Hoover stuck along with the cabinet, thinking something would show up, and it did. It was the Mississippi Flood. It was like old times to be doing something after being idle with the Government for so long. He did a wonderful bit of work and saved a lot of lives. But when they got 'em all dried off, and looked at them, they were Democrats. Well he didn't know whether to keep 'em or shove 'em back in again. But he was a humanitarian and he fed them and promised to take care of them until Congress would give them some flood relief. So it looks like he has them on his hands and the Red Cross's hands for life.

Now if that Flood had been in the North and it had been Republicans he had saved, why, he wouldn't have to charge it off to profit and loss. He could have wrung some voters out of it. But a Democrat voting for a Republican down South is just like throwing a hand full of gravel at a battleship. He will have their moral support, but their votes will go to a lost cause, as usual.

MARCH 15, 1928

The Democrats are having a lot of fun exposing the Republican campaign corruptions, but they would have a lot more fun if they knew where they could lay their hands on some of it themselves for next November. The difference in corruption in the two parties was 7,000,000 votes last election.

Been an awful lot in the papers lately about just who and what is to compose the New York Deligation to the Democratic Convention at Houston. At first they thought well, we will just go ahead and have the regular Deligates like we always have. Then someone got to thinking, "Well they wouldent be the right kind to use down there. The Kellys, Obriens and Donovans and Murphys and Isensteins and Levys and Gumbles. We got to dig up a different gang. Well they started in trying to figure out what style and manner of person to send.

They got to inquiring around to find out. But none of Tammany's Braves had ever been to Houston so they couldn't speak with much authority on just what type of Politician Houston was most partial to.

If they had just had some one who knew it would have been easy, for they have every style politician in the world.

So they started in with the basic idea that we got to send people that use their knife only when there is really something to cut.

"We got to kinder raid the social register and see if we cant cull a bunch that will know 'em off their seats in Houston with their social standing. Find people who have spent more time in a drawing room than they have in a caucus room. If a ward healer shows up and looks like he wants to go, knock him so unconscious he wont come too till after the Deligation have gone."

Try and find ninety Democrats that sleep in pajamas. Be sure there is ninety tooth brushes leave with the Deligation. Watch their language and dont let a sign of a dialect creep in. Now you may not get ninety of the above type who are boni fide Democrats, but fill out with what dissatisfied Republicans you can find. They will be so far from home that no one down there will know how they ever voted before.

But in the meantime the "Scouts" had come in and announced that they just couldent find ninety "High-brows," and that the Republicans that they approached all just through force of habit wanted too much of a fee. So it looked like the high hat idea had fallen through. It looked bad for a typical Tuxedo Deligation. So the Committee got off on another tack, they conceived an idea of trying to get some wealth mixed up in it. When they saw that Intellect was kinder short handed, they made offers to every well known wealthy man to loan his person to them for the duration of the Convention and make Al look like he was coming with the backing of "Big Business."

But "Big Business" was doing so good under Cal that nothing Al could offer them would make them switch. Cal had handed them everything but the mint, and they saw no way that Al could improve on that. But the "Steering" Committee was still resourceful. "Well we have fell down on Intellectuals, and Wealth. What could be the matter with sending some old Time Southerns, that loved the south so much they just couldent stand to stay there and see it suffer, so they moved to New York? You know the south is great on names and tradition, so we can round up a bunch of these old Babies that have still got their long coat, black hat and string tie."

The old Boys hadent been doing much since the Bar days closed, when they used to work off their Southern accent on poor unsuspecting visitors from south of the Montgomery and Ward line. They used to strike up an acquaintance, and before it ended the other fellow had paid for quite a snack of "Juleps."

You see the Committee was bound to not be represented by the regular voters. Not only the votes of their ninety deligates, but the impression of the Deligates was what they wanted to get over. Houston couldent possibly be hostile to an old decendant of Lee, or Jefferson, all of which could very easily be arranged by a little coaching on history before the Deligation started.

It will make the old Protestant boys realize that these are some of their own Countrymen after all, when they discover that they are not going to mass or Synagogue. "Why they are Christian folks, just like us; they dont go to Church anywhere!"

Course this New York Deligation can only represent them while at the Convention, because they perhaps havent registered to vote in New York for years. But if they make the Deligation look like something for just the duration of the Convention, why the experiment will have worked out O.K. Lot of the old boys will have to brush up on their southern accent. It's kinder rusty, and is a little overdrawn to what they will hear down south. But its a great idea, sending somebody who dont represent Hammany Hall. They are going to have the Deligates introduced to Smith after they get back from the Convention. They got 'em busy now memorizing the name.

April 21, 1928

I don't think Politicians are getting what is coming to them. They are lucky!

April 22, 1928

Corruption has supplanted the Tariff, as a National issue. But its awful hard to get people interested in corruption unless they can get some of it. You take a fellow that hasent received any corruption, and its kinder like the fellow that has never drank Sour Kraut Juice, he aint much interested in whether its good or bad. People just figure "Well there couldent be so much corruption, or some of it would have come my way." And the fellow that has received any of it naturally he is in favor of a continuation of the policy.

The Democrats were supposed to have started it in what was called Tammany Hall. But a good thing cant be restricted and is bound to spread. So the Republicans had their eyes open for all new wrinkles that would help them stay on the U. S. Pension list. So like everything else they took it and improved on it and brought corruption up to the high standard that it is today.

The Democrats always were a kind of a cheap lot. They never had much money to operate on. They were always kinder doing business on a shoe string basis. The type of Man they had with them went in more for Oratory than he did for Stocks and Bonds. They would rather make a Speech than a Dollar. They cultivated their voices instead of their finances.

You give a Democrat a high hat and a frock coat and put him on the speakers list, and he would turn down the chairmanship of the board of a big corporation. Give him a horse in the parade every year and that was just about all the glory he wanted.

The Democratic graft was mostly confined to sorter rounding the Saloon keepers into line with a Campaign collection every year. They thought that was just about the height of "Big Business." I guess it was because they dident know there was any other business. They dident know that a man that was owner of some mines, or lumber or coal, might also dig up something for the pot. (If promised a little break in the Tarriff, or Railroad rates, or suppressed opposition.) But their mind was on a Saloon and thats as high as they could elevate it. So the Republicans just was wise enough to see that the same principal applied to one business as to the other. If it was good for the Saloons to stand in with the Government, why it was good for all other business. So they commenced working out the idea in a big way. The men who were thinking of running for office got to looking 'round their various States and seeing what some other men wanted, and they went to them and said, "If you will sorter help me out at the poles, I think I can help you out getting these big things."

While the Democrat was still fooling his time away with the "Jitney" fellow the Republicans said, "There is only one way to be in Politics and thats to be in a big way. Whats the use of being a Piker?" So instead of getting a hundred dollars from some poor little Guy, they grabbed off a couple of thousand from the big fellows that was looking for something worth while, and they just kept working and building their business right up, till, look what it is today.

There is two types of Larceny, Petty and Grand, and the courts will really give you a longer sentence for Petty than they do for Grand. They are supposed to be the same in the eyes of the law, but the Judges always put a little extra on you for Petty, which is a kind of a fine for stupidness. "If thats all you got you ought to go to jail longer."

But the parties will never be changed as long as we live, for you cant change human nature. You cant broaden a mans vision if he wasent born with one. And another thing, its hard to get people to believe a thing as Corruption, when its something that has always been going on. These deals gradually come under the heading of legitimate Campaign business.

You promise something in return for something whether it is a Post Office, or an Oil well. Its what the Lawyers call "Sharp practice."

Its going to be awful hard to make an issue of corruption. Its like the poor, its always been with us.

If you promise a man that if you are made Senator, that he will be made a Judge, why you have sold him something. His votes have helped you to get your salary. You might promise him a river to get a damn built on, but you have always promised something, either directly or indirectly, and you cant get voters to distinguish the difference, *IF there is any.*

CHAPTER SEVEN

Republican Chautauqua, 1928

KANSAS CITY, JUNE 10, 1928

Flew in here yesterday morning from Chicago and made a forced landing on the backs of 21 Candidates, who were laying out in the grass on their stomack trying to figure out some way to stop Hoover.

The Propeller struck one in the head and that gave him an original idea.

He says, "Boys let's be honest with ourselves." Well, that was a laugh right there. "Let's don't kid ourselves. There just don't seem to be any prominent demand for any of us to be President, so what can we do?"

Well, just then the iron tail piece on the plane skidded off another so-called "Favorite Son's" head, and set him to thinking seriously, "Well, if nobody wants us, what do you say we all get together and stop the fellow that the majority want."

"That's a great idea," says all the rest in what sounded like unison. "What will we call our party?"

"Let's call it the 'Dog in the Manger Party.'"

"That's great. Now Members, can we trust each other?"

"We can till this Candidate is stopped, and then it's every fellow for himself."

"Now that's understood. We all sign an agreement that we won't start killing each other off till after we have killed the first fellow off. We are Gentlemen till our main mission is performed and then we revert to type. Is that plain to all of you?"

"It is."

"All right, Members, let's get to the Manger, and guard it with our lives."

"What's our slogan?"

"Keep the Party in the hands of Politicians."

"What's our Yell?"

"Three long growls."

Of all the Tips you get around here! Everybody has a different one. The Bell Boys where the Delegates are staying are the only ones that haven't got a tip since the thing started.

June 10, 1928

Today being Sunday (even in a political convention) I just got an idea I would see just how religious all these politicians really are, as I had heard that religion might play some part in the Fall festivities. So I grab a cab and rush from one church to the other all over town, and not a single candidate, or delegate, or even alternate, was among the worshipers.

Still, this Fall, in the campaign, you will hear them get up and shout "Our religion is the bulwark of our great and glorious country; we must continue to be God-fearing people; our Church is our salvation." Well, our churches are our salvation, but some of those babies won't be among those rescued.

JUNE 11, 1928

Well, I just got tired milling around the Hotel Lobbies all this time and I just made up my mind to go right where the Convention was being held. So when Andy Mellon come I just headed for his quarters. He had always been mighty nice to me and laughed at my little Jokes at the Dinners. So he had a Senator who was acting as a Doorman let me right in. To make sure that I would get in I took my tax receipt with me to show him that I did all I could to make his Department make a good showing, for I knew how hard he is trying to make us forget Alexander Hamilton.

"How are you, Mr. Mellon, the whole town has been waiting for you?"

"Hello, Will, I am glad to see you. How is your personal Campaign getting on?"

"I am doing about as well as all the other Candidates here with the exception of the one that will be nominated. Who are your Pennsylvania Delegation for?"

"Well, I haven't told them yet."

"If Hoover will keep you in your present job will you be for him?"

"Certainly, but he hasn't said that he would."

"Would you like to be President yourself?"

"No, I care not who is a Country's President, just so I can handle its money."

JUNE 12, 1928

We met this morning for no reason, and adjourned for the same. When Andy Mellon come in, everybody stood up, as though a lady had entered the room. Rather an effeminate move I thought.

The best thing at the convention was Schuman-Heink singing. Oh, what a grand old lady she did look, and how she sang!

I wish she had sang Fess's keynote speech.

I think we will have the boys out of the hotels by Thursday, so let's go on to Houston, where they at least know how to fuss.

If you are interested in Vice Presidents and such things you will be interested in this Convention.

Nobody in the history of Conventions ever saw a Convention start and end so quick.

The Politicians "Stopped Hoover." They stopped him from being Secretary of Commerce.

If you haven't had a room to stay in while here, you can get one now. There is six Candidate Headquarters that are to be sublet.

The Convention opened with a Prayer.

It was a Keynote Prayer. If the Lord can see his way clear, to bless the Republican Party the way it's been carrying on, then the rest of us ought to even get it without asking for it.

Then they brought on Simeon D. Fess. He delivered what is called the Keynote Speech.

A Keynote Speech is Press notices of the Republican Party written by its own members.

Here are just a few of the things that I bet you didn't know the Republicans were responsible for: Radio, Telephone, Baths, Automobiles, Savings Accounts, Law Enforcement, Workmen living in houses, and a living wage for Senators.

The Democrats had brought on War, pestilence, debts, Disease, Bo weevil, Gold teeth, need of Farm relief, suspenders, floods, famine, and Tom Heflin.

He told of so much money that we had saved that I think if he had talked another hour he would have paid us a dividend.

Once I thought sure he was referring to "Our Saviour" till they told me, "No, it was Coolidge." The way he rated 'em was Coolidge, The Lord, and then Lincoln.

It was an impromptu address that he had been working on for only six months. He made no attempt at Oratory, he just shouted.

He dramatized figures. When he told how many million we had saved, his voice raised. But when our savings had reached the billions, why his voice reached a crescendo. All expenditure was spoken in an undertone.

They adjourned till tomorrow, for the sake of the Hotels. They could have finished this convention in ten minutes today.

Men who yesterday wouldn't allow their names to be associated with the Vice Presidency are today announcing they would consider being drafted.

Hoover is drawing plans for one of the biggest engineering feats he ever embarked on.

So it's all over But Hoover and Curtis.

JUNE 13, 1928

All we have done today is listen to Senator Fess explain what he forgot to say yesterday. It seems he left out Roosevelt's name yesterday and it took him all day today to Alibi for it.

The whole show has degenerated into nothing but a Dog fight for Vice President.

They have weeded the Candidates down now to just the following: 96 Senators, 435 Congressmen, and 47 Governors.

They say Dawes is flying here to keep them from sentencing him to another four years listening to the Senate without ear muffs.

Let's get out of here and go to Houston. They haven't even got Hot Dogs to sell in the Convention building.

Now Jesse Jones, don't you get high hat down at Houston and not serve any there.

There is nothing to do here when a Speaker comes on. You have to listen to him.

Reed Smoot from Salt Lake read what sounded like a cross between a Financial report and a World Almanac. He spoke heartily of prosperity, but our National deficit was still thirty billions when he finished. The crowd couldn't hear him and shouted for him to "Speak louder." Then when he did speak louder and they did hear him, why they got sorer than a boil and wanted him to speak low again. He brought up Nicaragua. But he left the Marines down there. He said that we would protect American lives down there, even if we had to send some down there to protect.

The Farmers that spoke received much applause, BUT NO MATERIAL RELIEF.

ON TO HOUSTON for Hot Dogs, and excitement with every speech.

If they had taken these four words out of the Dictionary, this Convention would have been over a week ago, "THE GREAT REPUBLICAN PARTY."

JUNE 15, 1928

Wow! She is all over, Hoover and Curtis. The Republican Party owed Curtis something, but I didn't think they would be so low down as to pay him that way. He used to be floor walker of the Republican Party on the Senate floor. Now he will be Timekeeper.

Another Preacher prayed this morning and had to read his Prayer. There hasn't been a one that could make an impromptu prayer. This one was Methodist, and he wanted us "to look to the Hills for wisdom" and here we were nominating Charley Curtis from the plains of Kansas, where a five foot ash heap would constitute a precipice. This Preacher prayed for Plymouth Rock. But it's Boulder Dam we are after now. There is no appropriation goes with Plymouth Rock.

I hate to say it, but the Women that spoke were all terrible. Well, they were pretty near as bad as the men, that will give you an idea how bad they were.

JUNE 17, 1928

Did you ever see a town after they had just finished sweeping out a convention?

The Republicans have all gone back home to collect. You know, they don't pay off till after you have voted.

CHAPTER EIGHT

Democratic Follies, 1928 Edition

JUNE 23, 1928

Here we are down here in Houston all getting set for another Dog Fight. I think we are going to have a lot of fun. There is always excitement at a Democratic Anything. Of course it don't look like there is any way to keep from nominating Al, but that don't make any difference, there is always something that will stir up an argument even if they all agree.

JUNE 24, 1928

Everything is as quiet, restful, and beautiful, you wouldn't think there was a Democrat in a thousand miles. Been here three days, haven't heard a cheer, a Band, an Argument, or even an echo.

I wouldn't stay for the thing, but I know that a Democrat is just like a Baby. If it's hollering and making a lot of noise, there is nothing serious the matter with it. But if it's quiet and still and don't pay much attention to anything, why that's when it's really dangerous.

The Kansas City Convention took the life out of this one in more ways than one. You know you wouldn't feel so good either, if someone had just announced to you ten days ago, that it was Tunney that you were to meet in the finals.

But there is bound to be some comedy coming and here is the reason.

Since Prohibition was unearthed nine years ago, there has only been one argument invented that a Politician when he is cornered can duck behind, and that is the old Applesauce, "I am for Law Enforcement."

Now the Republicans held their Convention first, and naturally they grabbed this lone tree to hide behind. Now that leaves the Democrats out in the open. If they say anything about Prohibition, they either got to say, "It ought to be modified," or "It shouldn't be modified." They can't duck behind the old "Alibi" tree, "I am for Law Enforcement," for there is only room for one back there, and a Republican is already hiding there.

If I had been the Democrats I would have held my Convention first so I could have grabbed that "Alibi" first, if I had had to hold it three years ago.

Now naturally, the logical thing to do if it was a "Legitimate" business would be to nominate with Smith another wet as Vice President, and also put into the Platform a plank on modification, and have the whole prohibition thing out, on a straight out issue, and let the Voters settle it once and for all. But Politics is not a "Legitimate" business, and they won't do it that way.

Why? Because they don't know if there is more Wet Votes, or Dry Votes. So they are afraid to take a chance.

So they will try to "straddle" the same way the Republicans did.

So, if these Boys are not shouting and singing down here, it's because they not only have a Convention on their hands, but a PROBLEM.

So there is bound to be some laughs, and they will be serious and Unintentional, which are the best laughs in the World.

JUNE 25, 1928

Say, listen, I want to give you a little tip. The minute you read this in the morning, run to the radio that evening and get the Houston Convention.

Now I know they are all terrible to listen to, ordinarily, but get the keynote speech of this bird Claude Bowers. I was the first one that suggested him for this job when I followed him at the Jackson Day Dinner in Washington last Spring. He is a bear.

You haven't heard the Republicans called anything till you hear this fellow – comedy, oratory, facts and sense. Shut off on all the others, but you will thank me for tipping you off to this guy. He makes the Republicans pretty near as bad as they are. That's how good he is. Yours for straight tips.

JUNE 26, 1928

There is a fine Rodeo show on here, and when I just cant stand looking more Deligates in the face I go out and look at the calves and Bucking Horses, and you know its a kind of relief.

The women drys here have a regular hall where they go and pray that no wet shall enter the Kingdom of Heaven. They forget that when women enter Politics, their prayers don't even mean any more to the Lord. They are just classed with Politicians.

A Band of Women hailed me yesterday and wanted me to write something about helping them get "Equal Rights." So I told 'em I thought myself that they had too many, and it was mighty nice of them to want to split some of them with the men.

The whole talk down here is Dry. The Delegate just can't hardly wait till the next bottle is opened to discuss it. Prohibition is running about a quart to the argument here now. The South say they are Dry, and by golly, if the Bootleggers don't rush on some more mighty quick, they will be.

Tammany Delegates were coached and instructed not to drink while here, and they are the lonesomest looking Gang you ever saw. They all say, "Why pick on us to be the only sober ones here?"

Everybody has on a linen, or palm beach suit, not white, but it was once. If perspiration was a marketable commodity, the party could pay off the National deficit. The Rice Hotel lobby is so packed I have reached up and mopped three other perspiring brows before I could find my own.

There is a nice cool breeze blowing outside all the time, but nobody will go outside. It looks like all a Convention is, is just to sweat on each other. The lobby is so crowded that part of the New York Delegation can't say a word. And badges. If all the badges were laid end to end, they would reach the White House.

Was up in Barney Baruch's room last night. He was busy unpacking his blank checks, getting ready for the deficit. Admiral Dr. Grayson was with him. We talked till daylight of the times when Presidents were Presidents.

Was at lunch with Mrs. Woodrow Wilson at Jesse Jones' roof home on top of one of his cloud ticklers. Wonderful place. The only home I have seen to beat it was Waite Phillips' Buckingham Palace in Tulsa, Oklahoma. Mrs. Wilson looks wonderful and is as pleasant and charming as ever.

The principles of the Democratic Party were never listened to with more heated brows and perspiring necks than is paying its bodily tribute here. Have perspired for Jefferson, sweated for Jackson, fainted for Tilden and am dying slowly for Smith. I don't know that we are helping democracy, but we are certainly perspiring for it.

June 26, 1928

The Show was called to order at twelve twenty, Jeffersonian time.

It took 20 minutes of steady hammering to get order enough for them to listen to a prayer. They didn't want to listen to a prayer. It was an argument that they wanted to listen to. If I was Chairman of a Democratic Convention, when I wanted it quiet, I would announce, "Just one moment, Hyenas, if you will be quiet we will start a debate, and it has the possibilities of ending in a fight." That will shut 'em up in a minute.

The meeting didn't hold long. It was the shortest Democratic gathering on record. Some man prayed, I didn't get his name, or political faith. But from his earnestness, I should say he was a Democrat. He not only asked for guidance, but he wisely hinted for VOTES.

A Lady sang. Say, she was good. The only thing stopped her was a man made a motion to adjourn. She had on an awful pretty big picture hat. I imagine from the way she was dressed that she kinder figured that she might be called on.

She opened up with the Star Spangled Banner. She had a Dandy voice, and she knew the song, she didn't read it. People applauded her for knowing the words, and before you knew it, she just started right in singing another one, ad lib too. It was America. She did that because a lot of people don't know which is our National Air, America, or the Star Spangled Banner. So, being a good Democrat, she just took no chances on the party losing through not singing the right song, so she sang 'em both, and good, too. Well, when the audience realized that she knew all these old Folk songs, they applauded and by Golly, she knocked 'em off "Dixie." Well, Dixie in Texas is just as sure fire as a Flask.

H. L. Mencken, the undesirable element of Literature, was sitting by me and he suggested she follow it with "Marching through Georgia." I knocked him under the press table, before Captain Hickman, my Texas Ranger friend, could get out his gun to totally dispose of him.

But the big event was tonight. You know, I have been telling you all the time about this fellow, Claude Bowers.

I thought Jim Reed could denounce. Why Jim's denouncing would be taken as compliments after this Baby got through.

It wasn't a Keynote speech. It was a "Lock and Key" Speech, and after he had finished, why the whole Republican Party should have been put under Lock and Key.

It must be true, or they could sue him. Course him just being an Editorial Writer, he hasn't got anything. But Barney Baruch, and Jesse Jones, and Kenny, and Norman Mack, and them, they have got a little left over from the Democratic Administration, and they put this fellow up to saying it. Why if I was a Republican, I would be ashamed to go to the polls and collect for my votes after that.

June 27, 1928

The Democrats always do the unusual. They come here with the reputation that they never can get a convention finished, and here we are at one and its main problem is how to keep the thing going till Houston gets its flag money back.

Smith has been practically approved on the floor of the convention three different times, and Joe Robinson for Vice President once. Still they won't go ahead and have it done officially. We are all just sitting here waiting for the benediction.

The platform it looks like they will adopt is wet on week days and dry on Sundays.

This morning they got me out of bed early to attend a big Breakfast given to over a thousand Political women who have left their Husbands bed and Board and are assisting in America's champion pastime. I was the only *alleged* man at the breakfast. Just think of that, the only Male party invited to attend the principal Social function of the female contingent. Well, the old "Sheik" (I mean Sheep) of Claremore, Okla., sure did look his best in the only "seasucker" suit I had worn since a Baby.

These women are a great audience, when you get 'em off to themselves and speak to 'em in their native tongue. Us Women sho' had some fun.

Sam Blythe who sits by me in the Convention, and the best Political Writer that ever lied for a Candidate, told me that out of fifty years going to Conventions that this was the prettiest and best Hall he ever saw. Odd McIntyre was here with us. He was sitting with Sam and I, but he had to go back to New York to wash the Dog.

Last night Claude Bowers ended up his speech with the following:

"The Battle hour has struck. Then to your Tents, O, ISRAEL." That was to get the Jewish vote, but I never saw one living in a Tent.

Well, I have finished my mission at Conventions. Finally, a Preacher prayed last night, from memory and not from manuscript, and funny thing it was my old friend, Dr. Jacobs, of Houston, and he is a Cattle man in the week days. He raises Brahama Cattle, and Presbyterians.

If it wasn't for paying our respects and a few more days Hotel bills to Houston, why the thing is over.

So Voters, get in the middle of the road. Don't sell your

vote too cheap, for this is one Campaign where the Democrats will have as much money as the Republicans. Smith has as much backing as Hoover. So hold out for the highest bidder.

Tammany Hall has got more money than the Engineers Club.

"Unbutton your Purse, O ISRAEL."

JUNE 28, 1928

Senator George rallied the drys about him last night. But when they left the Hall and the Smith delegates got their corkscrews working, George was left stranded on a pile of emptys higher than the Convention Hall.

Franklin Roosevelt, a fine and wonderful man who has devoted his life to nominating Al Smith, did his act from memory.

Franklin Roosevelt could have gotten far in the Democratic party himself, but he has this act all perfected, and don't like to go to the trouble of learning something else.

It was a fine speech. It always has been, but it's always been ahead of its time. Now he has 'em believing it. The only part I didn't agree with is where he said that Al was "Good to Women, and Children, and Dumb animals," and he insinuated that the Republican President and nominee were not.

Now Franklin, you are wrong about the Republicans and the Dumb Animals. They just thrive on Dumb Animals. They are like Lincoln with the poor. They must love 'em for they have so many of them in the party. And I even believe that the Republicans like children. Not perhaps as children, but they are the material of which voters are made in a few years. So I believe the Republicans would be kind to 'em just so they would grow into manhood quicker.

I have heard so much at this Convention about "Getting back to the old Jeffersonian principles" that being an amateur, I am in doubt as to why they LEFT THEM in the first place.

All you hear about here is the amount of graft and corruption. But each man wants to put his Nominee where it is going on. Why if these offices are as bad as they say they are, I wouldn't want a decent friend of mine to even want to go in them.

They are stalling with the Platform, and when it is ready there is not a wire walker in America that can stand on it.

It's got to a point here now where State Delegations will "caucus" on a half quart.

JUNE 28, 1928

Let's see, this is Thursday. The elevators in the hotels are going up today.

Democracy has found a candidate. Now they are looking for a drink.

JUNE 28, 1928

Well Boys, she blowed up about noon today in a blaze of harmony.

Joe Robinson of Arkansas got the nomination [*for V. P.*] with more Democrats agreeing than had ever agreed on one thing in the history of the party. They got a great fellow in Joe. He is a real two fisted he Candidate. He comes from the wilds of Arkansas, where they are hard to take. I have had one in my house for twenty years, and there is just no managing em.

Lord, I have looked at enough Badges, and heard enough speeches that if I ever hear another man say, "The Grand old Republican Party," or "Back to the Jeffersonian principles," I will go to the gallows with a clear conscience. I just want to go back home, and go to sleep for a month.

All the Speakers said, "We are making History." Well, I don't want to be disrespectful to either party, but I am just tired of seeing history being made.

Goodbye, Houston, take care of yourself. But don't ever bid for another one of these things. You might get it.

Come on, Aeroplane, let's show these delegates how to travel.

If they could just hold the election now, before they have time to go home and think up something to call each other!

CHAPTER NINE

"We Are the Yaps, Not Them"

In this campaign the Republicans concentrated on "prosperity" with a slogan of "a chicken in every pot and two cars in every garage." It was also the campaign in which Al Smith's membership in the Catholic Church and his being a "wet" finished doing what the Ku Klux Klan and sectionalism had already started — splintering the Democratic Party so that when it was again brought together — under the leadership of FDR — it wasn't the same party at all.

JULY 8, 1928 [*on the conventions*]

Our Public men take themselves too serious. It just looks like they are stoop-shouldered from carrying our Country on their backs.

And the Women, poor souls, when they are allowed to speak, it seems they have paid more attention to the material in the dress than they have to the material in the speech. They mean well and act awful sincere. But the girls just aint there. It gets em out and gives em a chance to get away from home, and wear badges. But it just seems like they haven't added anything constructive to the art of Politics.

I think they take it too serious. I believe they would go further if they kinder ridiculed and kidded the men. They can do that in everything else, so why cant they do it in Politics?

Personally I think the Camera has done more harm for Politics than any other one faction. Every body would rather get their picture than their ideas in the paper. What does the platform of a Political party amount to compared to the photography! There is 10 cameras to every plank in the platform. Speakers get up early in the morning not to find out how their speech was received by the Press, but how the Pictures turned out.

A woman seconder of somebody's nomination would rather have her candidate lose the election than to have missed the front page in the morning holding a bunch of American Beauties in her arms.

But its a great game, this Convention game is. You cuss yourself for sitting day in and day out and looking at such nonsense. But the next four years find you back there again. So its really our mental exhaust.

JULY 12, 1928 [*on appointment of John J. Raskob*]

Say, did you notice who the Democrats grabbed off for stage manager. They are finally getting some sense and quit trying to appeal to the poor people with poor people. They figured let us grab off some rich man and make our party look like somebody had something.

There is nothing impresses the "common folks" like

somebody that ain't common. This fellow Roskob took General Motors when it was nothing but a few bent axles and some old carburetors and put it on Wall Street and got away with it. Now, if he can combine all the loose nuts of the Democrats he is liable to repeat.

Yours, for money in politics.

JULY 14, 1928

They say practice makes perfect at anything. But I tell you, Taint so. No nation that was ever invented under the sun does as much practicing "Talking" as we do, and if you think we are perfect at it, you just listen over the radio, or worse still in person to the speeches at these Political Conventions.

Even the man that I had touted to all of you as being a world beater, Claude Bowers, the Democratic Keynoter, fell down on me. At the Jackson Day dinner in Washington, he was a Bear. He was new and unknown, and nothing depended on it, but his getting a free meal, and he knew he would have received that before he delivered the speech.

He knocked em cold there. But he had a far different kind of speech. He said the same things at both places but at the dinner he did it more with ridicule, and sarcasm when he hopped on Republican corruption.

But at Houston he took it serious, and was trying to convict em, while at Washington he was only trying to indite em, and at the dinner he had a lot of comedy spread all through the speech, while at Houston there wasent a sign of a laugh all through it. He should have kept the good Gag of Kin Hubbard [*Abe Martin*] that he quoted and gave credit to. It was, "Old Abe Pash come to town the other day and bought a new pair of boots with money that he had saved up from the Wilson Administration."

That would have been a yell, and incidentally covered the whole prosperity thing better than all the hollering and preaching and quoting statistics that he could have done in an hour.

Maybe in the old days speeches were just as idea-less. But they was only being listened to by the Deligates, and the man making the speech was a Deligate, so he only had to appeal to intelligence as high as his own.

But nowadays this radio thing has changed all that. They are not just talking to a lot of politicians; they are talking to the world. And people are getting wise to the type of man that is supposed to be saving our Country right away he compares the intelligence of their talk with the talk that he hears in other lines of business, and it just don't stand up.

A speech nowadays is just like bootleg liquor. Nobody knows what all the junk is they put in it, but everybody knows that it just dont stand up. It tastes terrible and sounds worse. So lets dont hold another Convention till someone can think of a New Speech.

August 12, 1928

I didn't think Hoover would accept but he did. He says every man has the right to ask the following question: "Is the United States a better place for the average man to live in because the Republican Party has conducted the Government eight years?" If we are privileged to ask the question, I will be the first one to bite. *Is it?*

AUGUST 12, 1928

According to the Republican press of the country, Hoover's speech ranks right along with Washington's after-dinner effusions and some of Lincoln's monologues, but according to the Democratic press it was just another Republican press clipping and is in a "Class with all Presidential seconding speeches."

But as an independent I could see much truth and novelty in it. He was against poverty and favored education, even if you couldn't get into a fraternity. He said prohibition was a noble experiment, and he believed in noble things, even if they were only experiments.

AUGUST 17, 1928

From now till November neither of the boys can be themselves. They are on parade. They are eating and sleeping in a show window. They are acting every minute.

Coolidge is the only one nobody ever knew when he was acting and when he wasn't. He was like a ukelele. You can't tell when somebody is playing one or just monkeying with it.

AUGUST 20, 1928

Smith, when he accepts on Wednesday night (as he probably will) I bet he will tell how he and Tammany used to lay awake at nights just to think up ways to help the farmer and skin the city slicker.

Yours in sympathy for those that fall for this.

AUGUST 28, 1928

I don't know much about politics and nothing about religion, but I do know that since General Motors have gone Democratic that my Buick won't pull a hill, and it is the same hill that it used to go up on in high before Raskob went into politics.

SEPTEMBER 6, 1928

Politics are receiving a lot of attention because we have nothing else to interest us. We don't have to worry about anything. No nation in the history of the world was ever sitting as pretty. If we want anything, all we have to do is go and buy it on credit.

So that leaves us without any economic problem whatever, except perhaps some day to have to pay for them. But we are certainly not thinking about that this early.

Yours for more credit and longer payments.

OCTOBER 2, 1928

Al Smith unanimously nominated Franklin D. Roosevelt today for Governor of New York.

Roosevelt will always be remembered as the man that any time as many as three persons met, either in conference or convention, would arise and nominate Al Smith for President. You could just wake him in the middle of the night and he would start to nominate Al.

His nominating days over, he is now going to take up politics seriously. He is a Roosevelt by blood, but a namesake politically. If he had retained his splendid qualities and stayed with the Republican end of the family, he would have been President, but I doubt if he could have retained those qualities and been Republican.

OCTOBER 24, 1928

I hope the Democrats win this election just for one thing. I have heard 5,000 hours of "speeches" on a "return to Jeffersonian principles," and I want to see what "Jeffersonian principles" are.

Is it just an oratorical topic, or is it an economic condition? I know that Jefferson was for the poor but in his days that was good politics, for practically everybody was poor.

Of all the "dumb" issues that candidates bring up to try and influence people how to vote, I think "prosperity" takes the cake. How a speaker can convince a man that he is prosperous when he is broke, or that he is not prosperous when he is doing well, is beyond me. If a voter can't feel in his pocket and see if he doing well without having some total stranger tell him, then this Government shouldn't be in the hands of the people. We might as well have candidates argue with us that we have a pain in our stomach.

OCTOBER 31, 1928

Well, the promising season ends next Tuesday, and at about 8 o'clock that same night the "Alibi" season opens and lasts for the next four years.

To show you what campaign promises amount to, can you remember back a few weeks ago when the promise was made on both sides that "the campaign was to be run on a high plane"?

This campaign ends Tuesday, but it will take two generation to sweep up the dirt.

NOVEMBER 4, 1928

I have been studying the two parties and here is the difference: Hoover wants all the drys and as many wets as possible. Smith wants all the wets and as many drys as he can get. Hoover says he will relieve the farmer, even if he has to call Congress; Smith says he will relieve the farmer even if has to appoint a commission.

Hoover says the tariff will be kept up. Smith says the tariff will not be lowered.

Hoover is strongly in favor of prosperity. Smith highly indorses prosperity.

Hoover wants no votes merely on account of religion. Smith wants no votes solely on religious grounds. Both would accept Mohammaden votes if offered.

Hoover would like to live in the White House. Smith is not adverse to living in the White House. In order to get in there either one will promise the voters anything from perpetual motion to eternal salvation.

NOVEMBER 6, 1928

The election ain't over till 6 o'clock tonight, but it's been over since last June. Just think, We got people in this country that have to wait till votes are counted before they know.

This is going to be the greatest lesson in geography that New York City ever had. They never knew how many people live west of the Hudson River.

NOVEMBER 7, 1928

Would like to sell, trade, dispose of or give away to right parties franchise of what is humorously known as Democratic Party. Said franchise calls for license to enter in national elections; said right or franchise is supposed to be used every four years, but if intelligent parties had it they would let various elections go by default when understood they had no chance.

If in right hands and only used in times when it had an "issue" or when Republican Party had split, think it could be made to pay, but present owners have absolutely no business with it. Under present management they have killed off more good men than grade crossings have. Address Raskob, back at Chevrolet workshop.

NOVEMBER 8, 1928

Offers pouring in all day for the purchase of the Democrats. All want the title, but no one wants any of the cast.

NOVEMBER 11, 1928

Well it's all over, and what a relief! What has it proved? What has it profited us? We have gone through the most exciting and bitter election that we have ever held in our history. And what's the answer?

Friends have been turned into enemies, families have been split, husbands have choked wives, and wives have attempted to murder husbands, all because one wanted one Guy to draw a Government salary and the other member wanted the other fellow to live easy for the next four years.

I told you not long ago that the campaign lasted only a few months but that it would take two generations to sweep up the "Dirt." I think now that it is all over and we have a chance to sum up, I think I was too modest in the time, it looks like we will be hearing from this one as long as they keep historys in the Libraries.

You will please pardon a Comedian for lasping into seriousness, but there was no more reason for all this religious gab, and all the threats of what would happen if certain things were brought about.

There is no other line of business that any of them could get in where they would get one tenth part of the publicity that they get in public office, and how they love it! Talk about Actors basking in the limelight! Say an old Senator can make an Actor look like he is hid under a barrel.

You announce tomorrow that you will either take away a public mans salary or his Publicity and position, that he can have the choice of which to give up, and 90 percent will say take the salary away. They will find some way of living, in fact they will live on the strength of somebody calling them Judge, or Congressman, or even Alderman. Those old Babies like it.

Then all this yapping about Parties. If a man could tell the difference between the two parties he would make a Sucker out of Solomon for wisdom.

This country runs IN SPITE of parties, in fact Parties are the biggest handicaps we have to contend with. If we dident have to stop to play Politics any administration could almost make a garden of Eden out of us. If we were run by the Manager form of Government we would soon be paying so little taxes we would be lonesome.

You could transfer the Senate and Congress over to run the Standard Oil, or General Motors and they would have both things bankrupt in two years.

No other business in the world could afford to carry such deadwood. But we got em, and they are going to live off us someway, so we just as well put long tail coats on em and call em "Statesmen." They are great Guys personally, and they know in their own heart that its all a lot of "Baloney," and if they are smart enough to make us feed em, why then we are the Yaps, not them.

DECEMBER 5, 1928

My November message on the "State of the Nation": The nation never looked like it was to face a worse winter — birds, geese, Democrats and all perishable animals are already huddled up in three or four States down South. We are at peace with the world because the world is waiting to get another gun and get it loaded.

Wall Street is in good shape, but Eighth Avenue never was as bad off.

The farmers are going into the winter with pretty good radios, but not much feed for their stock.

I dont want you to think this message is pessimistic. Mr. Coolidge is an optimist, and will be till March 4.

DECEMBER 6, 1928

If the Democrats had had the party incorporated and listed on the Exchange as "Democratic Hopes and Aspirations, Inc." then let somebody buy ten shares to get it started, millions would have bought it on the Exchange that wouldn't think of taking it at the polls. They buy anything there worse than Democrats.

DECEMBER 11, 1928

If your side lost don't take it too much to heart. Remember there is always this difference between us and Italy. In Italy Mussolini runs the country. But here the country runs the President.

CHAPTER TEN

Will Takes Over the Democrats

JANUARY 1, 1929

Nothing much in papers today but optimistic predictions of all prominent men who are doing well.

Mr. Coolidge: "I look for nothing but prosperity through January and February."

Mr. Hoover says: "I look for things to kinder drag along in a haphazard way till about March, then real prosperity will start and continue for four to perhaps eight years. After that there may be depression."

JANUARY 19, 1929 [*in the* Saturday Evening Post]

Dear Al:

I like you Democrats; you are sorter my kind of people, but I am just sick and tired seeing the whole thing mismanaged. So I have decided to take it over and see what we can salvage out of it. But you got to take my advice from now on.

If I see fit not to start an Entry in '32, why we wont start any. I am tired seeing good men killed off for nothing; I am tired seeing one Party that is not One Bit better than the other, just Continually outsmart us. Those

Guys can be beat but Not with Jeffersonian and Jacksonian principles.

If a national question comes up, there is no sensible reason why we shouldent be on the Popular side, instead of the Right side all the time. Leave old Political Leaders in the Senate, where they can't do anybody any good or harm. Hide 'em when a campaign is on. They been making the same speeches since they was weaned.

There is absolutely millions of people in this country who are not even half pleased with the way these Republicans run things, but they prefer 'em to the Democrats' old-fashioned ideas. Now, taken out from under the influence of a lot of these old Mossbacks, you are a pretty progressive fellow, Al, and with you and this Fellow Roosevelt as a kind of nucleus, I think we can, with the help of some Progressive young Democratic governors and senators and congressmen, make this thing into a Party, instead of a Memory.

Get Raskob back on those Chevrolets again. He may know what Wall Street is going to do, but none of those Guys have got a vote. We don't need a Financier; we need a Magician.

February 17, 1929

Our Preachers are doing principal Legislation for us now. We pick up a Paper and it says, "We cant get this bill through because Bishop So-and-So is against it," and "We have to pass this as the Federated Parsons of Ossawatomie are behind it."

A Preacher just cant save anybody nowadays. He is

too busy saving the Nation. He cant monkey with Individual salvation. Every Cross road Minister is trying to be a Colonel House.

The Church is in Politics more than the Politicians. If Congress met on Sundays, why there would be no services anywhere. All the Ministers would have their eyes on Congress. We got to trust somebody to run our Country, and when we elected 'em why lets let 'em alone and see how they do. Then if they dont do why throw 'em out when they come up for re-election. But dont stand in the wings and prompt 'em all the time; that keeps 'em nervous and besides they never do learn their parts.

February 18, 1929

Ain't it funny how many hundreds of thousands of soldiers we can recruit with nerve. But we just can't find one politician in a million with backbone.

February 28, 1929

No wonder Hoover can't get a Cabinet.

Big men won't take it for they won't take a chance on a Senate insult. If he has ever earned more than a Senator, he is in League with big business. If he ever drove a Standard Oil truck, or was a bookkeeper in a Morgan bank, he is in league with monopolies. If he is independently rich, he is in league with the devil.

But if he has never done anything, and been a financial failure at that, he will pass the Senate as a brother, and every time Hoover finds a man of that type he is a Democrat.

And that's another stanch rule. You can't use even an

able man from the other party. That would revert to democracy, and not politics.

MARCH 15, 1929

This is income tax paying day. There is going to be no attempt at humor for it would be mighty forced. By the way, did you charge off money given to the Democratic campaign? You could, it's legitimate charity, not organized but a charity nevertheless.

MARCH 30, 1929 [*in the* Saturday Evening Post]

We are gathered in festive array at Chili Joe's Greasy Spoon, celebrating my appointment as Manager and Supervising Director of the Great Democratic Party.

The Republicans have run the Government and made money out of it for themselves. Now what we got to do is to show the people that we can run it cheaper for them. In other words, we got to cut the Republicans' price. It's simply a mercantile business in town—that's all the Government is.

Now the Republicans are established, they got the main store there. We got to come in, open up, and show the people we can give 'em as good or better goods at lower prices. Now, we, in order to do that, might not make as much out of it for ourselves as they are making, AT FIRST, but we have all got to kinder sacrifice immediate profits to what we can get when we really get going good. You see, they are bound to have people in this town that, while they are buying from them now, and have been for years, yet they are not satisfied. They would go to somebody else quick if somebody else had something to offer them.

But we can't come in and open up the Store with the same old goods we used to have when we used to run a little Store years ago. We can't sell 'em cotton stockings, button shoes, calico, Horseshoe Tobacco and snuff. We got to sell 'em scented Cigarettes now.

There is not five homes in any town now with a place for a fellow to spit. So we either got to swallow our tobacco juice or change with the times. You can no more sell a man Jeffersonian Principles than you could sell him a Croquet Set. He don't know what they are.

If it happened that many years ago, and you have to explain 'em, why, they couldent 'a' been much good.

A jug of Apple Jack and a chaw of Tobacco don't interest him along the hospitality line now. What he wants is a couple of shots of Rye, a niblick and the address of a friend.

Then your Women vote is a-coming in today. So can that old long-Underwear stuff and show 'em some Step-Ins that are prettier than the Republicans'.

You think they are a-buying "Glorious Tradition" at the Polls? No, Sir. They want to know what kind of a break they are going to get in Commerce and Industry.

They are no smarter than their Mothers were, but they think they are. Somebody humorously told them that they "swung this last election" and they foolishly believed it. So that will just whet their appetite for the next one.

Women, Liquor, Tammany Hall – all had their minor little contributing factors one way or another in the total, but the whole answer was: We just dident have any Merchandise to offer the Boys that would make 'em come over on our side of the Street. Our Ads consisted of enumerating the poor quality of the goods of our opposition, but we wasent offering any longer lipstick for the same money than they was.

MARCH 31, 1929

You know Women are getting into more things that are embarrassing to men. You see the first idea of giving them the vote was just to use the vote. But the Women contrary-like they are, they wasent satisfied. They started to take this equality thing serious. They figured "While we may not be as good as a Man, we are at least as good as a Politician." So the Scamps commenced to want to get in on the loot.

As soon as they found out a Political Job took no experience to hold, that it only took experience to get, why they commenced to make themselves rather embarrassing around the Political Employment bureau.

It was all right with the men when the women took the little Committee assignments where there was NO salary connected, but when they started to want to put their powdered nose into the feed trough, why that brought on complications. Now they are wondering, "Was the Womens vote worth what they are asking for it?"

Its not only that way with Tammany, but its getting that way all over. Women that used to wouldent think of gossiping anywhere but over a back fence, now wont say a word about you till the meeting has been duly called to order. Its scattered Scandal around more; its brought it more into the open; its changed lots of things around. Families that used to dident know there was a Restaurant in town are looking over the Menu cards on days when the Ladies' Auxiliary of the "Pork Barrel Society" is in session.

To us fellows that are not in Politics we are tickled to death to see the Women folks dealing such misery to the Politicians. And in the long run its good for humanity. Every job a Woman can grab off it just drives another Politician to either work or the poor house.

This Nineteenth Amendment is worrying more people in the Country than the Eighteenth. Its not only caused millions of men to go hungry (by their wives being away at a rally) but it is causing a lot of them to go jobless, all because the whole thing was a misunderstanding. The men give 'em the vote, and never meant for them to take it serious. But being Women they took the wrong meaning and did.

JULY 6, 1929

Today I read where a speech that Franklin D. Roosevelt had made had just about threw him in the ring as the next Democratic candidate.

Now there is a fine man. In fact, that is one of the characteristics of the Democratic party, that they have had some of the finest men as candidates that we have in this country, and it's almost a shame that they are to be eternally handicapped by being "right but never President."

But you can start now trying to dig up something and in three years you won't have found anything wrong with Franklin D. Roosevelt outside of being a Democrat.

NOVEMBER 1, 1929

Mr. Hoover is becoming a typical American President by becoming disgusted with the Senate early in his Administration.

Distrust of the Senate by Presidents started with Washington who wanted to have 'em courtmartialed. Jefferson proposed life imprisonment for 'em, old Andy Jackson said "To hell with 'em," and got his wish. Lincoln said the Lord must have hated 'em for he made so few of 'em. Roosevelt whittled a big stick and beat on 'em for six years. Taft just laughed at 'em and grew fat. They drove Wilson to an early grave. Coolidge never let 'em know what he wanted, so they never knew how to vote against him, and Mr. Hoover took 'em serious, thereby making his only political mistake.

CHAPTER ELEVEN

A House of Cards

Late in the fall of 1929 Republican Prosperity proved to be on paper. With the stock market crash, paper values took a dizzy dive into a bottomless abyss. Hoover, with his engineer's mind, tried to dam up the social, economic and political flood, a continuation of the same revolutionary forces which had brought on World War I, with an engineer's dam. He just wasn't the magician needed.

NOVEMBER 19, 1929

America already holds the record for freak movements. Now we have a new one. It's called, "Restoring Confidence." Rich men who never had a mission in life outside of watching a stock ticker, are working day and night "Restoring Confidence."

Now I am not unpatriotic, and I want to do my bit, so I hereby offer my services to my President, my Country, and my friends around Old Trinity Church, New York, to do anything (outside of serving on a Commission) that I can, in this great movement.

But you will have to give me some idea where "Confidence" is, and just what you want it restored to.

DECEMBER 1, 1929

You take confidence, its one of the hardest things in the World to get restored once it gets out of bounds. I have helped to restore a lot of things in my time, such as cattle back to the home range. Herded Folly Girls toward the stage door near show time. Helped to revive interest in National Political Conventions. Even assisted the Democrats in every forlorn pilgrimage, and a host of other worthy charities. But I tell you this "Restoring Confidence" is the toughest drive I ever assisted in. When I took up the work, confidence was at a mighty low ebb, that is so all the Papers and speakers was saying.

Wall Street had gone into one tail spin after another. You would pick up a paper in the morning and read the stock report and you wouldent think there was that many "Minus" signs in the world. Well the effect of it was just like going to Monte Carlo, and hearing that everybody was betting on the Black, and the Red had been coming up continually for two days. That would just simply demoralize southern France and the whole Riviera. Well thats what this Market was doing here. It was just taking all the joy out of gambling. If it kept on like that it would discourage Gambling and that, of course, would be bad for the country (Thats what they said).

Course there was a lot of us dumb ones that couldent understand it. We said, "Well if somebody lost money there, Why somebody else must have made it. You cant just lose money to nobody, unless you drop it somewhere and nobody ever finds it." Then they said a good deal of the money was "Lost on paper." That is it was figures but it wasent real money. Well I had done that. I could remember every contract I would get for a seasons work on the stage or screen, my wife and I would sit down and figure out what all we would have by the end of that season. Well at the end of the season we had the figures but we couldent find the money. So Wall Street Men had nothing on us. In fact I dont think it had anything on anybody, for we all can take a piece of paper and if you give us enough pencil we can figure ourselves out a pretty neat little fortune in no time, so when I heard that most of the money had been lost on "Paper profits," why I felt right at home with them.

But then everybody said it would have a demoralizing effect on the country for so many to have their paper Profits all rubbed out at once. That it would have the effect of making people more careful with their money, and thereby make it bad for speculation. That if people dident trade in stocks why Wall Street couldent exist.

So I says what can we do for 'em so they will keep on existing? "Why restore confidence." And thats what I been doing for weeks, writing and talking.

Course I havent been buying anything myself. I wanted to give all the other folks a chance to have confidence first. There is none of the greedy Pig about me. This confidence was for sale and I wanted them to have the very first chance of buying it.

I discovered the following:

Confidence hasent left this country; confidence has just got wise, and the guys that it got wise to are wondering where it has gone.

DECEMBER 20, 1929

I always felt there was only one thing that could possibly defeat Mr. Hoover's capable management of our affairs and that was when he run out of practical men to put on commissions, and sure enough he is getting shorthanded. Yesterday's commission dident have a practical man on it. Every one was a college professor.

It's to find out "what has brought the social changes in our lives here lately." Knowing college professors he gave them three years to agree on an answer.

I could have told him before sundown what's changed our lives: buying on credit, waiting for relief, Ford cars, too many Republicans, Notre Dame coaching methods and two-thirds of the Americans, both old and young, thinking they possessed "it."

JANUARY 10, 1930

Since the Wall Street crash, which the Republicans refer to as a "business readjustment," prominent men had done nothing but tell us the strength of the country.

We have been "stronged" to death in speeches and statements, but last night Mr. Coolidge said, "The heart of the American people is strong," and here over 500 died of heart failure during the late "Republican readjustment."

What he really meant was that "the American public's head is strong but his heart is weak."

FEBRUARY 21, 1930

On account of us being a democracy and run by the people, we are the only nation in the world that has to keep a government for four years, no matter what it does.

March 17, 1930.

We used to think that "prosperity" was a "condition." Now we find that it is a "commodity." Mr. Hoover has ordered it delivered to us in 60 days, same as you would a sack of flour or a side of bacon. If "good times" is not laying on our doorsteps May 15th, 1930, we can sue the Republican Party.

September 7, 1930

There is going to be a lot of changes in Washington when the boys gather after the next election.

Democrats are going to make some big gains for the people are sore at Hoover because they had to go back to work and couldent just make a living by buying a stock and selling it to the other fellow at a raise.

October 24, 1930

There has been more "optimism" talked and less practiced than at any time during our history. Every millionaire we have has offered a speech instead of keeping still and offering a job.

Our optimism is all at a banquet table where everybody there has more than they can eat.

November 16, 1930 [*after off-year elections*]

Well all I know is just what I read in the papers, and all I have read in the last week is about the Democratic uprising of November 4th. It was my birthday and the Boys of the party really did themselves proud in my honor.

The Republicans were looking for a punch in the jaw, but not for a kick in the pants at the same time. Why there was men beat at this wake that thought they had a deed on their seat.

Joe Robinson is mighty liable to be the Democratic Nominee in '32. It will be between him and Franklyn D. Roosevelt, and they are both mighty fine men. Joe if they want a dry, and Roosevelt if they want a wet. But the wets seemed to kinder swamp everything at this meelee and are gaining strength every day, so in '32 it looks like the wet Candidate will have the edge at the Nomination.

Looks like the Democrats nominated their president yesterday, Franklin D. Roosevelt.

JANUARY 6, 1931

I dont want to discourage Mr. Mellon and his carefully balanced budget, but you let this country get hungry and they are going to eat, no matter what happens to budgets, income taxes or Wall Street values.

Washington mustent forget who rules when it comes to a showdown.

JANUARY 15, 1931

Congress yesterday turned down the 15 million food bill and passed 15 million "to improve entrances to National Parks." You can get a road anywhere you want to out of the government, but you can't get a sandwich.

If you live under a Government and it dont provide some means of you getting work when you really want it and will do it, why then there is something wrong. You cant just let the people starve, so if you dont give 'em work, and you dont give 'em food, or money to buy it, why what are they to do?

What is the matter with our Country anyhow? With all our brains in high positions, and all our boasted organizations, thousands of our folks are starving, or on the verge of it. Millions of bushels of wheat are in Granaries at the lowest price in twenty years. Why cant there be some means of at least giving everybody all the bread they wanted anyhow?

Here they are starving in Arkansaw and in our adjoining State of Oklahoma they are feeding their wheat to the stock to try and get rid of it.

But the main thing is we just aint doing something right, we are on the wrong track somewhere, we shouldent be giving people money, and them not do anything for it, no matter what you had to hand out for necessities, the receiver should give some kind of work in return. Cause he has to eat just the same when he is laying off as he is working. So every City or every State should give work of some kind, at a livable wage so that no one would be in actual want.

Of course it would cost the Taxpayers more money, but if you are making it, and all your fellow men are not why you shouldent mind paying a good slice of it for the less fortunate.

Course the big mans argument, and all the heavy Taxprayers alabi, is that when you take too big a slice from a man as taxes it takes that much more out of his investments and might cut down on money being put into enterprises. But it dident work that way after the War, and during it. Why Income taxes run as high as seventy percent on every dollar earned, and yet there was more money being made and put into things than there is now.

If your Income Taxes go to help out the less fortunate, there should be no legitimate gick against it in the world. This is becoming the richest and the poorest Country in the world.

Why? Why, on account of an unequal distribution of the money.

How can you equalize it? By putting a higher surtax on large incomes and that money goes to provide some public work, at a livable wage.

There is nothing that makes a man feel better than to know that no matter how bad things break he has something to fall back on, that he can make a living out of. It would be a glorified Community Chest idea, only instead of it being doled out to you as Charity you would work for it. There would never be any real Unemployed. The so-called unemployed would be working for the State or Government a guaranteed number of hours each week, at a living wage.

Now that we got that settled all we have to do is to get it by Congress and see if the Republicans will vote a higher Income tax on the rich babies.

It might not be a great plan, but it will DAM sure beat the one we got now.

MAY 31, 1931

President Hoover made a speech Saturday at Valley Forge. He found somebody that was worse off than we are but he had to go back 150 years in history to do it.

JUNE 28, 1931

Will you do me one favor. If you see or hear of anybody proposing my name either humorously or semi-seriously for any political office will you maim said party and send me the bill.

A comedian can only last till he either takes himself serious or his audience takes him serious and I dont want either one of those to happen to me.

I wont run no matter how bad the country will need a comedian by that time. I couldent run anyhow because I cant make up my mind which side to run on, "wet" or "dry." I dont know which side the most votes is on and I cant straddle it for that's where all the rest of the candidates are.

What is there to worry anybody over the next nominations anyhow? It's one year away but the candidates will be Hoover and Curtis versus Franklyn D. Roosevelt and some Western or Southern Democratic Governor.

I have looked politics and the movies both over and while they have much in common I believe politics is the most common, so I will stay with the movies. It's hard to give up the old White House but it would be much harder to take politics seriously.

So long, Boys, the first ex-candidate.

AUGUST 15, 1931

Ten men in our Country could buy the World, and ten million cant buy enough to eat.

OCTOBER 25, 1931 [*radio broadcast*]

We used to be told that depression was just a state of mind but starvation has changed that impression. Depression is a state of health. It's moved from the mind to the stomach. And it aint really depression either; it's just a return to normalcy. We are just getting back to earth. We are back to two-bit meals and cotton underwear and off $1.50 steaks and silk under rompers. The trouble is America is just muscle bound from holding a steering wheel. The only place we are calloused from work is the bottom of our driving toe.

This country has just got one problem: it's not the balancing of Mr. Mellon's budget (that's his problem); it's not the League of Nations; it's not the silver question; not a one of those problems mean a thing in the world to us *as long as we have seven million of our own out of work*. Our only problem is to arrange the affairs of this prosperous country (yes, prosperous right now) so that a man that wants to work can get work and give him a more equal division of the wealth the country produces.

Now if our big men in the next year cant fix that, well they just aint big men, that's all.

What does prohibition amount to if your neighbor's children are not eating? It's food, not drink is our problem now. We were so afraid the poor people might drink, now we fixed it so they cant eat.

We got more wheat, more corn, more food, more cotton, more money in the banks, more everything in the world than any nation that ever lived ever had, yet we are starving to death.

We are the first nation in the history of the world to go to the poor house in an automobile.

Our potter's fields are surrounded by granaries full of grain. Now if there ain't something "cockeyed" in an arrangement like that, then this microphone in front of me is a mousetrap.

Now a miracle can't happen and all these people get a job over night. It's going to take time. So they must be fed and cared for perhaps all winter.

Every one of us that have anything got it by the aid of these very people. There is not an unemployed man in the country that hasent contributed to the wealth of every millionaire in America.

The working classes dident bring this one. It was the big boys that thought the financial drunk was going to last forever and over bought, over merged and over capitalized.

Now the people are not asking for money. They are asking for a job. But there is no job, towns and cities cant say they havent got the money. For the same amount of money is in the country as when these folks had their share. Somebody's got it.

Last winter we dident realize the need. But this winter we got no excuse. Its been shown to us all summer.

Now dont wait for the government to feed these people. I have seen lots of audiences and heard lots of appeals, but I have yet to see one where the people knew the need, and the cause was there, that they dident come through. Even Europe who hates us and thinks we are arrogant, bad-mannered and everything else, will tell you that we are liberal.

Dog-gone it, our folks are liberal. I dont know anything about America's being "fundamentally sound" and all that after-dinner "hooey," but I do know that America is "fundamentally generous."

OCTOBER 27, 1931

Well, this was Navy Day. We celebrated it this year by lopping off its appropriations. Wake up some morning with a war on our hands, then the mad rush will be on to build battleships, give the companies big bonuses to get 'em done quick. Then we will have to go through that silk-shirt buying period again.

NOVEMBER 23, 1931 [*to FDR*]

I got your letter about the Patient from Claremore. Now I will take care of that myself. I will send this Party down to your place and see if it dont help em.

Now we got the "Slightly" ailing taken care of, what are we going to do about the serious cases, The Democrats?

They been at *Hot Springs* for ten years.

I withdrew and named you as the beneficiary, and now I dont know if that support which I threw to you will do much good, but anyhow I am turning HIM over to you.

If people in 32 are still as hungry as they are now, and from the looks of things they will be "Hungrier," why the Democrats have got a fine chance.

They only vote for our Gang when they are starved out, we fatten em up and then they turn Republican again. If

I get east anyways soon, I am coming up to see you. From what I hear, you seem to be keeping impeachment from the door. Thats harder to stave off than the wolf nowadays with most Governors. Well good luck to you, and Mrs. Roosevelt, and your troop.

Meet you at the convention anyhow. Looks like Reno will get the next one.

JANUARY 10, 1932

Since the big epochal gastronomical meeting of Democrats nobody knows what Al and Franklin D. Roosevelt has been saying to each other. But it's about like this: "Listen Al, give me a chance. I been nominating you for years. Now you do the nominating and let me do the running. Won't you? Come on, Al, be a good fellow."

"Now, Frank, just give me one more crack at 'em. Then if I don't do anything, why you can have 'em. I had tough luck last time. Hoover was hot. But he has cooled down now and I believe it's my year. So just give the old boy one more crack at 'em, won't you, Frank? That's a good fellow."

JANUARY 22, 1932

See where Congress passed a two billion dollar bill to relieve Banker's mistakes and loan to new industries. You can always count on us helping those who have lost part of their fortunes but our whole history records nary a case where the loan was for the man who had absolutely nothing. Our theory is to help those who can get along even if they don't get it.

FEBRUARY 12, 1932

This is an election year. Every statesman wants to vote appropriations but is afraid to vote taxes. The oratory of Washington is on "reconstruction" but the heart of Washington is on November fourth 1932.

FEBRUARY 24, 1932

You cant get a room in Washington. Every hotel is jammed to the doors with bankers from all over America to get their "hand out."

I have asked the following prominent men in America this question: "What group have been more responsible for this financial mess, the farmers? labor? manufacturers? tradesmen or who?" And every man – Henry Ford, Garner, Newt. Baker, Borah, Curtis, and a real financier, Barney Baruch – without a moment's hesitation said, "Why, the bankers."

Yet they have the honor of being the first group to go on the "dole" in America.

APRIL 20, 1932

Talk about economizing and cutting out all unnecessarys. What's the idea of holding the Chicago Republican Convention?

This morning's papers announced Mr. Hoover's campaign plans, the route, the towns, who he would shake hands with, and what he would wear.

And as for the platform, it will be the same one they have read for forty years but have never used. And the speeches will be the same ones delivered for forty years but never listened to.

April 28, 1932

Conventions will be on us now. They are like the locusts. They come every few years. Will meet you all there, at one or the other of 'em. It will be good Conventions this year for both sides will be in doubt.

June 6, 1932

We never realized that elections were so near till we see by the papers this morning that each political party has "some" plan of relieving the unemployed. They have been unemployed for three years and nobody paid any attention to 'em. But now both parties have discovered that while they are not working, there is nothing in the Constitution to prevent them from voting. So Democratic campaign leader "hooey" and the Republican leader "baloney" say: "We have to do something about this. Miss Secretary, reach in the bag and get out some of those old campaign promises. We will dust 'em off and use 'em again this year. And remember no matter what the other side promises, see their promise and raise 'em two more."

CHAPTER TWELVE

The Democrats Rallied

June 12, 1932

Well here I am right at the stage door waiting to see all the actors in this great comedy called "a convention held for no reason at all." I have the distinction of being the first Democratic white child to arrive at the Republican fiasco. Breakfast at home Saturday morning, dinner in Kansas City, then into Chicago for breakfast Sunday. But disgraced myself by making the last hop on the train, as there was no regular plane. Guess I am getting old and going back. Be taking up golf next.

A newspaper man spoiled my whole convention by asking me if "I was an alternate." Now a delegate is bad enough, but an alternate is just a spare tire for a delegate. An alternate is the lowest form of political life there is. He is a parachute in a plane that never leaves the ground.

June 13, 1932

The wet lobbyists have taken the whole convention. They give you a badge and a drink. Lot of us dont know what to do with the badges.

Mr. Dickinson of Iowa is the "Keynoter" and he has the toughest job of any one of them ever. If he "points to accomplishments" he is sunk, and if he "views with alarm" he is sunk. So we are just liable to get two solid hours on the weather.

Charley Dawes is the most popular man in town. He still has a bank that is open.

JUNE 16, 1932

Well the old Republican Convention of 1932 went into either history or the ashcan at three-thirty this afternoon.

Its the same old vaudeville team of Hoover and Curtis. They nominated Hoover but after a tough fight.

18 thousand out of nineteen thousand yelled for repeal last night but the one thousand had the vote.

Last night was a real session. It sounded like something but thats because there was 12 thousand Democrats in the galleries.

Democracy and the right of free speech that you hear so much about had a setback there today. Ex-Senator France wanted to withdraw his own name and propose the name of Calvin Coolidge for President. Well that machine just bundled him right up and threw him into the alley. That was the real sensation of the convention.

See you at the Democrats where they will let anybody nominate everybody.

CLAREMORE, OKLAHOMA, JUNE 17, 1932

Well I was the first Democratic white child to escape from the Republicans. Just flew in here from Chicago in four hours.

JUNE 19, 1932

Mr. Hoover says he is not going out and lectioneer for the job. Thats kinder like a pitcher saying, "I dont need to even warm up against this team."

CHICAGO, JUNE 25, 1932

Well here we all are gathering in for the roundup of the Democrats. They are coming into Chicago by plane, train, Fords, buckboards and on burrow. The Texas deligation arrived on Burros headed by that fearless old statesman Amon G. Carter, the genial dirt farmer of Shady Oaks, Texas.

Amon is National Committeeman, deligate, alternate, steering wheel, banker, receiver and wet nurse for the Texas deligation. They have taken over the Sherman Hotel and have generously allowed the California deligation to spread their bed rolls out in the halls, so they can stand guard over the Texas deligation.

Oh, say this will be a convention. Of course the old Republicans did the best they could with what little they had to work on. We did have some fun at that. Would have had more if they hadent "bulldogged" that fellow France who wanted to nominate Coolidge.

Chicago is going to do herself proud just like she did with the Republicans. The last day of the Republican show they killed 4 gangsters for the amusement of the deligates and I know being a Democratic city at heart she will do as much for the Democrats. One of those they bumped off was named "Red" somebody and he was an alternate for Capone.

Jewett Shouse is here guiding the destinies of the Roosevelt forces. All you can hear is "Will they stop Roosevelt?" Well they dident stop him from getting six or seven hundred deligates. But maybe they can get 'em to change their minds after the deligates have seen some of the other candidates and maybe some of the others will switch to Roosevelt after they have seen face to face their own candidates. Anyhow its a good spot for a deligate to be in. Never was a deligate so much in demand. I am sorry that I dident "del." I had a chance in California. They wanted to make me one. Only I think they discovered I had none of the qualifications of one.

June 26, 1932

The plan is to "stop" Roosevelt. Then everybody "stop" each other at a time when the Democrats should be "starting." They are trying to change the "two-thirds" rule. It takes two-thirds to change it. If two-thirds of the Democrats agreed, they wouldent be Democrats. Cant change it. The hotel men are against it.

Al Smith, always frank, said, "I am not only trying to stop Roosevelt, I am like the rest of 'em trying to stop everybody but myself."

Talked with Governor Byrd of Virginia, a very high class man which is practically his only handicap.

June 27, 1932

No convention today. If you ever saw a disgusted bunch of people leaving a hall, it was all of us today. Here people had travelled hundreds of miles, joined deligations, some come as spectators and paid fancy prices to see eleven hundred deligates sit there and act like a lot of Republicans. Why it made me almost ashamed I was a Democrat.

Shades of Thomas Jefferson, shadows of Andy Jackson and outlines of William Jennings Bryan, are we going to degenerate into a party of agreement?

Is it the influence of the female deligates that have ruined the reputation of the old "hell raising, rip snorting" Democratic Convention and made us spineless, in fact effeminate?

Shame on you. Now dont lets have another session like that one. Wake up tomorrow and get in there and fight. If a speaker says something, no matter if its right or wrong, disagree with him, chuck him out.

June 28, 1932

Ah! They was Democrats today. They fought, they fit, they split and adjourned in a dandy wave of dissension. Thats the old Democratic spirit.

A whole day fighting over what? A President? No. A Platform? No. "Well then what did they take up eleven hundred deligates and 12 thousand spectators time for?" Why to see whether Huey Long (the Louisiana porcupine) was to sit on the floor or in the gallery. Well the "porcupine sticks right on the floor." And the other four hours was fighting over who would be chairman of a convention thats already a week old.

You cant beat the old Democrats for comedy. Time means no more to them than to a Mexican "Burro."

The Democrats are the only known race of people that

give a dinner and then wont decide who will be toastmaster till they all get to the dinner and fight over it. No job is ever too small for them to split over. But you would a loved 'em today. They was real Democrats.

JUNE 30, 1932

Did the Democrats go wet? No, they just layed right down and wallowed in it. They left all their clothes on the bank and dived in without even a bathing suit. They are wetter than an "organdie" dress at a rainy day picnic.

The plank was made from cork wood nailed together with a sponge.

I just want to know what all these old dry office holders that went wet over night are going to tell those Baptist preachers back home. They going to say, "Father, I cant tell a lie. I saw the votes going and I had to go after 'em."

JUNE 30, 1932

You remember away back in the late part of 1927 I had a piece in the Saturday Evening Post asking Smith not to run that year; that things wasn't right; that anti-prohibition was growing but not enough. I told him that it was a Republican year and no Democrat could be elected; that anti-prohibition feeling would be strong enough in 1932 to put him over.

Well, you will pardon me for bringing that up now, but I just can't help it. Us folks that write are right so little of the time that we have to brag on these very rare occasions.

Well, if he had done that we would all have been home

two days ago. They would have nominated him on the first half-ballot this year and the Democrats would have "walked" in to the White House. What reminded me of this was last night Al spoke himself of being four years ahead of his time.

JUNE 30, 1932

Politics aint on the level. I was only in 'em for an hour but in that short space of time somebody stole 22 votes from me. I was sitting there in the press stand asleep and wasent bothering a soul when they woke me up and said Oklahoma had started me on the way to the White House with 22 votes.

I thought to myself, "Well, there is no use going there this late in the morning" so I dropped off to sleep again. And that's when somebody touched me for my whole roll, took the whole 22, dident even leave me a vote to get breakfast on.

Course I realize now that I should have stayed awake and protected my interest but it was the only time I had ever entered national politics and I dident look for the boys to nick me so quick. Course I should have had a manager but the whole thing came on me so sudden and I was so sleepy – I had been taking opiates all night, no man can listen to 35 nominating speeches and hold his head up, and I am sure some of these that did the nominating can never hold theirs up again.

Now I dont want you to think that I am belittling the importance of those 22 votes. They was worth something there at that time. Not in money, mind you, for there is not $2.80 in the whole convention. But they buy 'em with promises of offices.

I expect at that time Roosevelt's bunch would have given me Secretary of State for that 22. And I could have sold to Al Smith for maby Mayor of New York. Why I could have taken those votes and run Andy Mellon out of the embassy in England with 'em. I could have gotten that job with only ten of the votes.

And what do I do – go to sleep and wake up without even the support of the Virgin Islands. They not only took my votes but they got my hat and my typewriter. I not only lost my 22 deligates but woke up without even as much as an alternate.

Now what am I? Just another ex-Democratic Presidential candidate. There's thousands of 'em. Well, the whole thing has been a terrible lesson to me and nothing to do but start in and live it down.

JULY 1, 1932

Did you ever parade at 6 o'clock in the morning? Nobody ever did but the Democrats. I been in circus parades and Wild West parades, but I had never entered a political parade. I had laughed at many a one, but had never become looney enough to participate.

But this morning as dawn was breaking over the machine-gun nests of Chicago and you could just see the early peep of light down early rising gangster rifle barrels, one of Oklahoma's ex-Governors arose and started to put in nomination a fellow Governor. His melodious voice aroused me from my slumbers. It was a friend, Henry Johnston, nominating my old friend Bill Murray.

When he finished the heavens broke loose, noise accompanied by bedlam, and what dashes into the arena? Not as you would expect at that hour of the morning, a milk wagon, but a band of beautiful little girls, all dressed in kilts, and thank goodness, not playing bagpipes, but musical instruments.

They had come all the way from Oklahoma City to help "Our Bill" Murray's parade. Was I going to get in it? If I could get woke up I was. I had no hat. Brisbane had been sleeping on mine during the nominating speeches. So Amon G. Carter (whose farm is on the principal street of Dallas) acted as my unmounted outrider. He handed me a straw hat with the word "Texas" on the band, and for no reason at all (like Democrats do everything) somebody handed me a cane. I waved it till I almost hit Mrs. Woodrow Wilson in the eye. Along the route of march we picked up a couple of girls who had been stranded by some earlier demonstration. They evidently were just "thumbing" their way around the hall. I was against taking them on. But Amon thought perhaps they were maby F.F.V.'s from the old commonwealth of Virginia and were trying to make their way back to Gov. Byrd's headquarters in the Culpepper corner of the hall.

Then as if by magic the rising sun started creeping in through the stained-glass windows of this great cathedral of liberty and justice, and I got the first real look at our traveling companions. The heels of their shoes were much run down, which we knew at a glance was the badge of the Republican party. And then we realized that they were leftovers from the late Hoover uprising in the same hall two weeks ago.

Some kindly soul that had temporarily escaped the depression handed me a box of popcorn so I had rations through the biggest part of the pilgrimage. The hall runs about three miles to the lap. The journey got us no votes, but like all these half-witted convention parades, it kept anybody else from getting any votes, or rest either, until every marcher has become thoroughly disgusted with himself.

CLAREMORE, OKLAHOMA, JULY 3, 1932

Flew down here to recuperate from one straight month of speeches. Heard a mule braying awhile ago out at the farm and for a minute I couldent tell who he was nominating.

Roosevelt made a good speech yesterday and he did aviation the biggest boost it ever had. Took his family and flew out there. That will stop these big shots from thinking their lives are too important to the country to take a chance on flying.

It was a good thing the Convention broke up. Times was so hard some of the deligates had started eating their alternates. Cannibalism was about to be added to other Democratic accomplishments.

I have one thing to be thankful for. I am the only defeated candidate that dident have a band left on my hands to ship back home. Could an artist paint a more pitiful picture than a poor defeated candidate waking up the morning after the vote and seeing thirty five horn tooters that have on account of the human laws to be delivered back home? Its enough to discourage candidates but it never does. Four years later they are back again, same ones.

July 4, 1932

The Democratic Convention was a victory of the country boys over the city slickers. New York and Chicago come there thinking that on account of being uninstructed they thought they would be in a position to stop Roosevelt, sell out to the highest bidder and go home driving the bank wagon. Great idea. All that went wrong with it was that the old Orange Squeezers from California thought of it first, sold out and was on their way West with the loot before New York and Chicago "jiggilos" could get their cards marked. It was a lesson in rural politics.

July 5, 1932

There is more Democrats here in Rogers County, Oklahoma, running for office than in both Chicago's "fiascos." Looks like the taxpayers in the U. S. are the only folks hiring any help nowadays.

A private business when it dont do any business dont need anybody. But the less business the public has the more we hire to tend to it. There is but one county institution that needs enlarging and thats the insane place and put us all in there till we know enough to vote to cut out at least fifty percent of our governing expenses.

JULY 9, 1932

Now that the "Seances" are all over and I sit and think of the amount of "Applesauce" and "Hooey" that was spilled there you wonder that we are even doing as well as we are as a Nation.

When you think of thousands of people in a hot stuffy hall away up till the early morning hours listening to "The man I am about to nominate has the qualities of a Jackson, the Statesmanship of a Jefferson, and the homely common sense of an Abraham Lincoln." Then the next one nominated would have all these and then a couple more, maby the looks of McKinley and the oratory of Bryan. Hours on hours of that, then they would all get up and march around the hall, part would march and part would hiss.

But with it all they were a good bunch. I guess just so much of that has to be. I guess there is no profession as "Crazy" as politics. Its a profession all its own.

Of all the "Trades" and "Deals" and "Under Cover" happenings that go on during one of those conventions! A State Deligation is with "their" man, but are they? Maby their leaders have already sold out to some opposition man, and are to deliver to him after the next ballot is taken. They "Trade" all kinds of ways. Then the Deligations begin to slip sometimes without anyone monkeying with 'em.

Its just human nature to string with a winner. Thats what they call getting on the Band Wagon. They know they cant get any Post Offices out of the loser, so sympathy cuts no ice. They quit him so quick there is nothing left but the campaign buttons, especially at this last convention when there was a Presidential Candidate to every ten voters.

"Do these fellows really think they will get somewhere?" Sure they do. There is nothing that can kill hope in a candidate. He just thinks the breaks were against him that time, and that he will get it the next time.

But at that there is a lot of humor among them, and its not all unconscious. There is some pretty good kidders among our leading candidates and politicians. They kind of take it serious before the crowd but when they are kinder off to themselves in a little bunch why they can kid themselves as much as any one.

You meet some great folks at those conventions, Governors, ex-Governors, Senators, ex-Senators, all the names that you have become accustomed to in the past, and maby haven't heard of in a long time, why you find 'em at these conventions.

Its the Fourth of July celebration of national politics. Its a clam bake of big politicians. If they cant get on the deligation they come as mere spectators.

Then its becoming a great trip for the women. They slipped her the vote, and she slipped off the old Mother Hubbard and into the old "Organdie" and she is meandering her way through a solid week of gabbing. And having a great time.

But its a show that no American should miss. Its entertainment, and its enlightening. It gives us a kind of an idea that most men that emerge from it with any spoils, were more lucky than competent.

A good campaign manager can do more than an able candidate. "Trades" makes Presidents more than ability. But as bad as we are, and as funny as we do things, we are better off than the other Countries, so bring on more conventions. The bigger, the noisier, the crazyier, the better. No nation likes noise and "Hooey" like we do.

We are all cuckoo, but we are happy.

JULY 13, 1932

Here is a funny situation. The women Anti-prohibitionists said, "We will support the party that comes out for direct repeal." And they would if it had been the Republican Party. But as luck would have it, it was those "mangy" Democrats instead. Now most of these women are wealthy Republicans. And they are having a time now trying to get out of it.

They want prohibition repealed all right but not bad enough to repeal the Republican Party with it. They want it wet but not wet enough to be Democratic.

In other words politics is thicker than beer.

CHAPTER THIRTEEN

The Voters Feel in Their Pockets

JULY 14, 1932

Roosevelt has actually started his Presidential campaign. I see pictures all over the front page today of him fishing. Are we never to get an original candidate?

Well at least he dident stand in the creek with rubber boots on. This campaign will be settled on fish. Do you want a deep sea fisherman in the White House – flounders and cod – or a big trout and perch man?

AUGUST 1, 1932

This is not an election of partys or policies this fall. Its an election where both sides really need the work.

AUGUST 5, 1932

Every year it gets harder and harder to tell the difference between a Republican and a Democrat (course outside of the looks). But I believe I have found out the sure way to tell one from another this year. Its just the way they talk.

The Republican says, "Well things could have been worse" and the Democrat says "How?"

AUGUST 7, 1932

Been telling you for a year what these Republicans would do with that market just in time to knock the poor inoffensive Democrats out of their hard earned votes in November.

Now they are all just a buying and selling among themselves in stocks that havent shown a cent of increased earning power. That shows the thing is kinder "cockeyed." The earnings should come first and then the raise in price of the stock.

AUGUST 11, 1932

Yesterday farm machinery went up on the stock market. Now there is not a farmer in the U. S. that can pay his taxes, or his groceries. Now how is he going to buy any farm machinery? He has no more credit if he wanted to. He couldent get a garden hoe, much less a threshing machine. He can plow with a forked stick and raise more than he can sell. So that raise dont look so hot. Thats like Xmas trees going up at New Years.

SEPTEMBER 14, 1932

What do you know about Maine going sane? Why four years ago they imported a Democrat into the State just to show around at the fairs.

Even Wall Street got plumb discouraged at the news. "You mean to tell us this booming and trading we been doing among ourselves here has all gone for naught?"

Mr. Hoover wired to Everett Sanders, "Tighten the lines, enlighten the people, our cause is right."

Roosevelt just grinned, and even the original couldent a shown more teeth. The old campaign is getting hot.

SEPTEMBER 16, 1932

Roosevelt is headed West. Says he is just out to meet the folks. But he will give preference to anyone of legal age and a registered voter.

Mr. Hoover who originally wasnt going further west during the campaign than the Potomac, has started looking at time tables. Politicians in order to hold the real dyed-in-the-wool radio nut are crooning their speeches.

SEPTEMBER 26, 1932

The Democrats are attacking and the Republicans are defending. All the Democrats have to do is promise "what they would do if they got in." But the Republicans have to promise "what they would do" and then explain why they havent already "done it."

I do honestly believe the Republicans have reformed and want to do better. But whether they have done it in time to win the election is another thing. The old voter is getting so he wants to be saved before October every voting year.

BEVERLY HILLS, SEPTEMBER 30, 1932

Well Mr. Roosevelt has come and gone. Seemed mighty cheerful and happy. Thats one thing about a Democrat. They never as serious as the Republicans. They been out of work so long they got used to it.

The Democrats take the whole thing as a joke and the

Republicans take it serious but run it like a joke. So theres not much difference.

OCTOBER 5, 1932

I'll tell you Al and Franklin dident make up a day too soon. They going to bury the hatchet. Decided to bury it in Hoover.

OCTOBER 30, 1932 [*after going to South America*]

I have had the most terrible disappointment. I never do look at a Calendar and I naturally thought election come around the first day or so of November. So I was timing my South American jaunt to arrive back here after the speeches was over. And here I go and make a weeks mistake in my time and arrive back in the midst of the most collosal rodeo of applesauce in the history of our national pastime. I would have rather made a forced landing in the Andes. From now on you will never catch me without a calendar.

NOVEMBER 1, 1932

There should be a moratorium called on candidates speeches. They have both called each other everything in the world they can think of. The high office of President of the United States has degenerated into two ordinarily fine men being goaded on by political leeches into saying things that if they were in their right minds they wouldn't think of saying.

Imagine Mr. Hoover last night, "Any change of policies will bring disaster to every fireside in America." Of all the conceit. This country is a thousand times bigger than any two men in it, or any two parties in it. These big politicians are too serious about themselves and their parties. This country has gotten where it is in spite of politics, and not by the aid of it. That we have carried such political bunk as we have and still survived shows we are a super nation.

This calamity was brought on by the actions of the people of the whole world and its weight will be lifted off by the actions of the people of the whole world, and not by a Republican or a Democrat.

So you two boys just get the weight of the world off your shoulders and go fishing. Both of you claim you like to fish, now instead of calling each other names till next Tuesday, why you can do everybody a big favor by going fishing, and you will be surprised but the old U. S. will keep right on running while you boys are sitting on the bank. Then come back next Wednesday and we will let you know which one is the lesser of the two evils to us.

NOVEMBER 8, 1932

We thought when the radio was perfected and everybody could hear a speech, that it wouldent be necessary to drag a President around over the country like a circus. But, no, the State Leaders must satisfy their vanity by having him appear "in person" in their State. But after all, there is very little dignity, very little sportsmanship, or very little anything in politics, only "get the job and hold it."

NOVEMBER 8, 1932

This election will be over at sundown and let everybody pray that its not a tie. For we couldent go through with this thing again. And when the votes are counted, let everybody, including the candidates, get into a good humor as quick as they got into a bad one. Both gangs have been bad sports. So see if at least one cant redeem themselves by offering no alibis but cooperate with the winner, for no matter which one it is the poor fellow is going to need it.

So cheer up, lets all be friends again. For one of the evils of democracy is, you have to put up with the man you elect whether you want him or not. Thats why we call it democracy.

NOVEMBER 10, 1932

Well the returns are pretty much all in. All but Kentucky. They got a law they cant count their votes till everybody sobers up, so it will be quite a little bit before we get them.

I was surprised at the vote the Republicans poled in Mississippi and Louisiana. I thought there was more postoffices there than there is.

By the way what ever become of the Roosevelts that claimed they was only eighth couzins to this one?

NOVEMBER 12, 1932

The last campaign brought in religion. This one replaced it with fear. This time they tried to scare you into voting a certain way.

It takes a great country to stand a thing like that hitting it every four years. When you figure that you have a system where you make business stand still and people go nutty for three months every four years, why somebody who concocted the idea of election certainly figured out a devastating scheme.

The Candidates are "High Typed Gentlemen" till the contest gets close then the "Brute" comes out in 'em. What starts out to be a nice fight winds up in a street brawl.

But it all comes under the heading of Democracy.

And as bad as it is its the best scheme we can think of. So lets all rest up for '36, mow the grass out of the street, get that disaster out of those firesides, and start another battle over those Post Offices.

CHAPTER FOURTEEN

A New World Is Upon Us

NOVEMBER 14, 1932

Herbert has invited Franklyn down to see him. Now on the face of it that looks like the last word in hospitality. But lets look that gift horse in the face. Is Herbert just crazy about Franklyn? No, "Children," prominent men are never crazy about each other. Herbert's in a hole. But if Franklyn confers with him and then something is done why they split the blame 50–50.

NOVEMBER 25, 1932

If you think this Democratic victory brought on harmony, you just wait till they start to hand out those post offices down South. There will be more people killed in the rush than in the flood.

The old "Hide Bound" Republicans still think the world is just on the verge of coming to an end and you can kinder see their angle at that for they have been running things all these years.

NOVEMBER 26, 1932

The last few years under Mr. Coolidge and Mr. Hoover there had grown the old original idea of the Republican

Party that it was the Party of the rich. And I think that was the biggest contributing part in their defeat.

This last election was a revulsion of feeling that went back a long way ahead of the hard times. Mr. Hoover reaped the benefits of the arrogance of the party when it was going strong.

Well after that twenty eight election there was no holding 'em. They really did think they had "Hard Times" cornered once and for all. Merger on top of merger. Get two non-paying things merged and then issue more stock to the Public. Consolidations and "Holding Companies." Those were the "Inventions" that every voter that had bought during the "Cuckoo" days were gunning for at this last election.

Saying that all the big vote was just against hard times is not all so. They was voting against not being advised that all those foreign loans was not too solid. They was voting because they had never been told or warned to the contrary that every big consolidation might not be just the best investment. You know the people kinder look on our Government to tell 'em and kinder advise 'em. A many an old bird really got sore at Coolidge but could only take it out on Hoover.

Big business sure got big, but it got big by selling its stocks and not by selling its products. No scheme was halted by the Government as long as somebody would buy the stock. It could have been a plan to deepen the Atlantic Ocean and it would have had the indorsement of the proper department in Washington, and the stocks would have gone on the market.

This election was lost four and five and six years ago, not just this year. They dident start thinking of the old common fellow till just as they started out on the election tour. The money was all appropriated for the top in the hopes that it would trickle down to the needy. Mr. Hoover was an engineer. He knew that water trickled down. Put it uphill and let it go and it will reach the dryest little spot.

But he dident know that money trickled up. Give it to the people at the bottom and the people at the top will have it before night anyhow. But it will at least have passed through the poor fellow's hands. They saved the big banks but the little ones went up the flue.

No, sir, the little fellow felt that he never had a chance and he dident till November the Eighth. And did he grab it?

The whole idea of Government relief for the last few years has been to loan somebody more money, so they could go further in debt. It aint much relief to just transfer your debts from one party to another adding a little more in the bargain.

No, I believe the "Boys" from all they had and hadent done had this coming to 'em.

DECEMBER 22, 1932

I dont want to lay the blame on the Republicans for the depression. They're not smart enough to think up all those things that have happened.

JANUARY 1, 1933

Ten million people have gone without work for three years just listening to "big men" solve their problems.

Question: Do you think world leaders can get us out of this?

They might, ignorance got us in.

Do you think we will get out of this depression just because we got out of all the others?

Lots of folks drown that's been in the water before.

Why this administration wants to stick in there till the last dog is hung is hard to understand. It's like a troup of actors getting hissed off the stage, but insisting on staying on there because they had a two weeks contract.

This is not only the lamest lame duck Congress, but it's our last lame duck Congress.

It's a mighty inspiring example of just how honery a Congress can be, if they really make up their minds to be honery. We just got about seven more weeks of show and then these boys go into what some writer has termed oblivion. Oblivion is a one way ticket down.

FEBRUARY 6, 1933

The lawmakers can pay more homage to a President in death, and deal him more misery in life than happens in any civilized nation.

After a fine oration on Mr. Coolidge's achievements, we listened breathlessly for fear some Senator would get up (just out of force of habit) and denounce the oration as being "partisan, misleading and made in the interest of the opposing party."

FEBRUARY 21, 1933

Every man, every industry in the United States was hit by depression. Before you start dealing out public funds to help, you should first find out if we have enough money to give part of them a sandwich and leave the rest to go hungry.

But, no, they didn't do that. They just started right in by helping the bankers, so every man, woman and child in the U. S. thinks, and rightfully, that they have got as much right to get some sort of government aid as the bankers, the railroads, and big business. They got the first U. S. dole, and it will never be finished till the last one hundred and twenty million reach in and get theirs.

The Rogue's gallery photograph show us that three of Roosevelt's cabinet escaped from the Senate. That's like going to the Old Men's Home to get athletes.

March 5, 1933

America hasn't been as happy in three years as they are today. No money, no banks, no work, no nothing, but they know they got a man in there who is wise to Congress, wise to our so-called big men. The whole country is with him. We have had years of "don't rock the boat." Sink it if you want to, we just as well be swimming as like we are.

You would never get a Republican Administration to voluntarily close a bank. Their theory is leave 'em open till they shut.

March 8, 1933

For three years we have had nothing but "America is fundamentally sound." It should have been "America is fundamentally cuckoo." The worse off we get the louder we laugh, which is a great thing.

And every American international banker ought to have printed on his office door "Alive today by the grace of a Nation that has a sense of humor."

If the Chase National turns "square" and removes itself from the security companies (that's the banks' roulette wheel) it will be a death blow to modern banking. Imagine a bank having to live on interest alone! Removing their security or holding companies is like taking the loaded dice away from a crap shooter.

MARCH 23, 1933

Nothing is as bullheaded as a party newspaper, be it Republican or Democratic. People are the first to forget party lines; newspapers are the last.

MAY 1, 1933 [*Gulf radio broadcast*]

Mr. Roosevelt has in his short time introduced some very great changes.

First he deloused Congress. That was a fertile field. When he got to the Senate he had to send for more disinfectant. He burned their clothes. Why today the U. S. Senate and Congressmen appear before us in almost a reverent light. Children can say, "My father is a Senator," and not have to duck when they do it. He has made it an honorable profession. In the old days a public office was based on oratory (and doubtful oratory at that); today it is based on obedience.

Where a Senator used to think he was a general; today he knows he is a private and when he is told to march right, march left, he does it. And he is a good private. Let the Commander-in-Chief be responsible for wrong commands. Roosevelt has shown that a Congressman is a cog in progress and not a rusty nail to puncture the tires of progress.

Why who ever thought they would live to see the day that they would look up to our lawmakers? But it has come. Why the rascals have become a public benefit and not a national nuisance.

MAY 5, 1933

Chamber of Commerce dinner in Washington was fine. The humorous part of it was that all the big manufacturers and producers in there had been all their life hollering, "Keep the Government out of business."

Well, my companion was Jesse Jones of the RFC who held a mortgage on every full dress suit in the house. There is not a business that the Government hasn't been asked to join. Nothing makes a man broadminded like adversity.

MAY 7, 1933

Now Mr. Roosevelt is on the air tonight. I have him following me. Generally I like to follow those big fellows when I speak for they generally expound a lot of logic and theories, so somebody has to come along and offset 'em with facts.

But Mr. Roosevelt is different. He is a terribly plain spoken man over the radio. Remember the wonderful speech that night about the banks. Long adjectives and nouns he dident mess with 'em at all. He knows that what the country wants *is relief and not rhetoric.*

He is the first Harvard man to know enough to drop

three syllables when he has something to say. Why compared to me he is almost illiterate.

His heart to heart talk about the banks only had one long word and that was sincerity. The speech was full of that. It changed the thought of a nation. Over night it switched us from takers out to putters in.

Unfortunately a banker cant pray (well, he can pray but no one with authority will listen to him). But if they could, they should thank Roosevelt, as well as interest, for their daily bread.

You will find history will record that speech as being the detour sign for depression. It was of the people, for the people, delivered so that confidence would not perish from this earth.

May 14, 1933

President Roosevelt is the only dictator by popular demand in the history of the world.

May 21, 1933 [*Will addressed the United States Senate.*]

The Senate will kindly come to order. Sit down there, Mr. Garner, I am running this night session of the Senate. And if you be right good I wont tell 'em you are the Vice President. You can stay awake tonight. This is one speech you havent heard a dozen times. And, Mr. Garner, I got some regular business for you. There is a little poker game going on.

Its lucky we are holding this session in the Grand Ball Room of this expensive hotel. It gives you Senators a chance to get in here for the first time.

Now listen we are going to have some order here.

Huey Long, quit prowling around there and sit down. If you got no place to rest yourself, Louisiana will gladly *dig* you a place. And dont even look like you want to make a speech.

Wait a minute. Here is a bill from the President. I dont know what its about and we will pass it with the usual procedure of not reading it. All those in favor say — EYE — all those opposed say NO. The EYE have it.

Hello, Alice, you will have to stand up there. We havent enough seats for the Democrats. I know he is your fifth cousin. I am Harry Lauder's but it never got me anything.

Now all you Republican members of the Senate get over there in that Jim Crow corner of the ball room. Be right still and nobody will notice you are here. Senator Hiram Johnson will you please make up your mind, are you going over in the Jim Crow corner or are you going to try to sit down here in front with the Democrats?

Pat Harrison, you and Senator Robinson of Arkansaw, quit deviling those Republicans. They have had a tough enough year as it is.

Borah, I have told you a thousand times I am not going to recognize Russia, not unless they shave.

I have just received another bill from the White House. I wont read it, but would like the usual vote. All those in favor say EYE — all opposed, the EYES have it.

The clerk just tells me the contents of that last bill we passed a few minutes ago, not that it matters to you, but it was to cancel the entire debt, and pay Europe for all the expense they had been out getting it cancelled, and we are to make them a loan equal to what they owed us. This last bill you just passed is to sink the navy, give Japan the Phillipines and Honolulu, take the Sam Browne belts off the Army, and have two weeks celebration.

Wait a minute. Here is a note from the Pres. He says read this. He tells me he cant think of anything else, so to adjourn the Senate, not only now, but forever. Wants you to go home, if you have the nerve or the fare.

Now the reason he is going to let you all go home is so that you can take with you the bills that you have passed this session. He wants you to read them. Now the President dont absolutely insist that you read these bills. If you have time, you can kinder look and see what you have done the past year. You may not be back with us again next fall.

There has been quite a bit of discussion between the intellectual end of our Government, representing Mr. Tugwell, Ezekiel and Moley, as to just whether they needed you boys back here again.

July 13, 1933

This fellow Roosevelt can close the banks, he can tell industry how much to pay, and how many hours to work, he can hold back the sun, he can evaporate the water. But when he demands that a postmaster has to be able to read, that's carrying dictatorship too far. He is monkeying with the very fundamentals of American political parties. I tell you this suggestion of his is bordering on treason.

The idea of a postmaster being able to read! It looks like an undemocratic move to favor the college man. I tell you he will ruin the Democratic Party. We mustn't let him get away with it.

JULY 18, 1933

Mr. Roosevelt, I dont think I need remind you that a signal sign saying "slow" on a street called Wall (placed there by you personally in order to let 500 essential industries catch up to them) would be appreciated by all other traffic headed for recovery. It wouldent be so bad but these are the same traffic violators who got too far ahead and gummed up our last parade.

SEPTEMBER 11, 1933

It looks like they are trying to get a little more conscience on the market, and a little less preferred stock. It's just decency by government control.

The farmer deserves a profit, but the guy that's not eating deserves a meal more. The stockholder deserves his dividend, but the unemployed deserves his job more.

OCTOBER 3, 1933

Now everybody is saying, Will we recognize Russia? Sure we will if they will buy anything.

In the A.F.N. (absolutely financially nutty) days we wouldent recognize Russia, for they had defaulted on their debts, wouldent go to church and were socialists. In fact in those C. D. (Cuckoo days) we were so cocky rich that we wouldent hardly recognize each other. But, Brother, it's different now. We are just looking for something to recognize. And debts, my Lord, if we dident recognize nations that owed us and dident pay, we would be a Robinson Crusoe on a desert island.

Russia might have been aetheists when we had money, but now that we are broke we aint going to let religion interfere with business. Some nations can come over that worship a golden calf but we will recognize them as long as they will buy the bronze from us to keep the old calf golden. We sell to the Chinese and they are heatherns, just like the Republicans.

Yes, sir, we are going to recognize Russia. We would recognize the Devil with a false face on if he would contract for some pitchforks. The shape we are in right now we would be glad to receive a good will tour from Alababa and his Forty Thieves, if they needed enough tooth paste and radio tubes. So bring on your Russia. We will trade 'em cotton for caviar and Junius Facial Cream for Vodka.

Nothing will bring a Nation off its moral high horse like poverty. Poverty is a terrible handicap but a great humanizer.

Speaking of finances, I have heard of a nation being frightened to death of a war, of folks worried to distraction over the health of their loved ones, of people uneasy of a threatened pestilence, but we will go on record as being the first nation that is literally scared to death over what will happen to its dollar.

This nation needs a more equal distribution of wealth. That's one thing the dumb guy knew before the economist. And I will say one thing for this Administration.

They may not get wealth equally divided among everybody. But they have done one thing:

It's the only time when the fellow with money is worrying more than the one without it.

NOVEMBER 20, 1933

Mr. Roosevelt was rather undecided exactly what to do on the stabilization of the dollar till the U. S. Chamber of Commerce came out and told him what to do. Then he knew exactly what to do. Do what the Chamber said not to do. Mr. Roosevelt knows he is right now, before he was in doubt.

NOVEMBER 24, 1933

Big headlines say that the big bankers to show Roosevelt his financial scheme dont suit them, they are unloading Government bonds by the bushel. He wont play their way so they are going to sell their ball and bat and get out.

I cant just recall, but as well as I remember, wasent they the fellows that the Government was helping so much not long ago?

DECEMBER 24, 1933

Well there is lots more good cheer this Xmas than last (or the last three), and it's not all out of bottles either. It's in the heart, in the confidence and in the renewed hopes of everybody.

Course there is an awful lot of folks that are not working, but they have never been the ones that's complained. Fear has never come from the fellow with no job, or no food. He has stood it wonderful. I doubt if a parallel will be found where millions hung on with such continued hope and patience as in this country. But I believe even the most down and out, while he might not see a turkey Xmas day, he can see one in the future.

DECEMBER 31, 1933

In years to come when all these professors switch from economists to historians, they are liable to label 1933 as the historical year, the year of the big switch, from worse to better. So, so long '33, panics come every twenty years, so we will be seeing you in '53.

JANUARY 4, 1934

Mr. Roosevelt proposed in his speech that the NRA and a lot of these other government regulated business ethics would be made permanent. Well that was a terrible blow to some business men. They had figured they would only be required to be honest by the government till the emergency was over.

JANUARY 6, 1934

A country is just like a family — love, arguments, fights, hates — and everything. But the one thing that does unite a family is illness. They can be poor as Job's turkey but they scare up a doctor, get a nurse, get medicine, no matter how poor. They always manage to get it, no matter how much of their future they have to mortgage. Expense is the last thing they think of. Save the life is the thing.

Now comes the big family — which is our whole country — some of the family have prospered, but most of them, like most of any family, have maby worked as hard, tried as hard, but due to just the breaks of the game, why they havent been able to weather the tide.

There is lots of sickness all at once, ten millions are out of work and that affects at least 30 million. That's a fourth of the family. They say it may take ten billion dollars for doctors and medicine.

It's paid to people who can only hoard it till they are able to sign their name on the check. And by the following Saturday night that money has changed hands 20 times. Then if we are not too pessimistic we hope that some of these patients will get well and get out from under the doctor's care.

This Roosevelt is a kind of a funny man, especially for a man that has been raised rich and associated with big men. Just through talking with him last week, I found the doctor bill wasent worrying him at all. And if I remember right, he has quite a little bit of taxable property. I just looked at him and thought to myself, "Well you got more to worry about if this thing busts than I have, and if you are not worrying I certainly am not going to."

So if you want my report on the condition of the country, I WOULD ADVISE YOU NOT TO GIVE UP YOUR CITIZENSHIP. For this man Roosevelt has got a kind of a nutty idea this country will amount to something some day. Queer fellow.

They are accusing Roosevelt of being a dictator. Well, a dictator is just like a parachute. They are made for a crisis. You can use one if you like, or you can jump without it. It may not open, but if not, you land right by the other fellow anyhow. He had faith that something "would grow wings for him before he came down."

FEBRUARY 17, 1934

Well got some social news for you. I am not so hot on the social gag, but back in Washington couple of weeks ago attended what they call a White House reception. Thats one of those little quiet intimate affairs where sometimes for homelike purposes they only have 12 or 14 hundred guests. At the bigger ones it runs up to a couple of thousand. It starts about nine oclock.

I pretty near had an argument with the President while he was changing from his tuxedo (which he had worn at dinner) to his dress suit which of course he would have to wear at the big Reception. He had asked me into his room to show me all the things he has in there. I asked him if he dident sit down during the time the people was passing by (It takes about an hour and half). Well he said, no, that he stood. Well then I blew up. I told him he ought to sit down. That was one time I was telling the President of the U. S. what to do. I have done it a lot of times but not so they could hear it, but this time I was laying the law down.

Well anyhow I dident get away with it. He went right down and stood up all that time. I dident win but I think I am right.

MARCH 27, 1934

Funniest thing in this controversy over a bill to regulate Wall Street. Wall Street now wants to write their own bill. They are pleading guilty, but want the privilege of pronouncing their own sentence.

MAY 18, 1934

Congress been laying awful low lately, so we better look out. You cant house five or six hundred men in tight together, and the heat coming on, without having some catastrophe being caused by it. Roosevelt knows that, and would personally pay their way home, if he could get 'em out.

CHAPTER FIFTEEN

The Honeymoon Wasn't Over

Many of the Republicans had been predicting — some of them with almost confidence — that the Roosevelt honeymoon with the people was over. The elections of 1934 — off-year elections — were the first test.

June 10, 1934

I am going to tell you something that hasent been brought up in public in years. I am going to say a few words for the Republican Party.

Spelled, R-E-P-U-B-L-I-C-A-N.

Your fathers and grandfathers will remember the name. The reason I know it's not been spoken of is that you cant speak of something unless you think of it and you cant think of it unless something happens to bring the name up. I got to thinking of the Johnston flood, the Galveston tidal wave, the Chicago fire, and my thoughts naturally drifted to the Republicans. Not that they were responsible for the above events, but there has been lots of people always been awful suspicious.

Now where has that Republican party gone? Such extermination of an entire race has never before been recorded. History records that they were rather a kindly people and were good to their young. Never warlike – in fact, they would step aside and egg the Democrats on till they declared war, then afterwards say, It was you that did it.

They were a thrifty race. Controlled most of the money. They had a certain foresight and would take over the reigns of government about the time things were going good. And when they saw pestilence and famine was about to be visited on the land, they would slip it back to the Democrats.

The Democrats were a kind of a semi-heathen tribe. They were a nomad race. They could live on little because they had never had much.

But they don't live on little when they get in office.

Their greatest traits were optimism and humor. You had to have optomism to join the Democratic Party and you had to have humor to stick with 'em. But they had a certain native shrewdness. They figured out that the one way to get the money away from the Republicans was to put a – bounty – or (as the Latin calls it) taxes on 'em.

Bounty or taxes is a thing you pay if you have anything, and if you havent you dont. Well, the Democrats knowing the Republicans had it, and knowing they dident, put it on 'em.

The theory was that while the Republicans are smart enough to make money the Democrats are smart enough to get in office every 2 or three times a century and take it away from 'em. And do these Republicans howl when this bounty—or taxes—hits 'em! They yowl like a she bear being deprived of its young.

And the Democrats are heartless. If they can get their hands in a Republican's pocket to get it out is just like trying to pull a badget out.

So the whole thing is just a revolving wheel. One party gets in and through a full stomach and a swell head oversteps themselves and out they go. And the other gets in. And that's as it should be. For there would be no living with one of 'em if they knew the other one dident exist.

Now the Republicans admit they are the rich ones, that they are smarter and can make money faster, so it's a good thing the old Democrats come along and level 'em off every once in a while. If they are so smart let 'em go out and make some more.

So they tell me that in quite a few places around over the country there is scattering Republican campfires. They are coming out of their caves and hidden valleys, director's meetings, and coupon clipping rooms and are sharpening up their campaign speeches to try and get back into the old teepees and post offices.

So that about concludes the bedside story of the two great Political parties which we work night and day to support.

June 6, 1934

Mr. Roosevelt has a unique position in the feelings of the people. They will let you throw a brick at him, but its got to be loaded with something besides political mud.

The President kinder held up for his brain trust. He

said he would take brains anytime in preference to politics. He just as good as admitted you couldent get both in the same body.

JUNE 26, 1934

Congressmen coming dragging in from Washington, some of 'em looking like they had hitchhiked. Now their real work starts, that is trying to get elected this Fall. I tell you its no easy life when you consider that battle to get back there. I just dont know what they are going to promise the voters this Fall. This is a tough time to think up something new.

JULY 1, 1934 [*after an FDR "fireside chat"*]

Now the question is, Are we better off than we were? Yes, we are, only thing is we were sicker than we thought we were, and we are just going through that weak spell following a severe illness. And we are astonished to find ourselves so weak, and we say, "Doc, my Lord, I must have been sicker than I thought. I cant even hardly move yet."

You see we are awful weak now because he has just operated on our heart (our gold) and when you take out our heart and start monkeying with it, we are always kinder leery as to whether you can get it beating again.

You see your gold, or your heart, has just got so many beats in it, and you go start trying to put in more, and you are fooling with life.

But we have confidence in him and he tells us that all this new form of surgery may work and that if it dont he will try some other. But what we are afraid of is that he may have to use another patient.

July 15, 1934

In the minds of the candidates the country is always "on the Brink." And your decision on November 4th will be the deciding factor on whether it goes on over the Brink, or if you wisely vote for me, I will grab it just as its going over and pull it back. The answer is in your hands.

Poor old "Brink." I dont know of anything we been on more of than we have it. We have tottered on the Brink so long and so much that I think the Old Brink has got hand holts on it. I am beginning to believe we wouldent go over it on a bet. We are what you call "Brink" conscious, so dont let the boys scare you about this "Brink" bugaboo. Its away overestimated.

September 18, 1934 [*broadcast from London after a trip around the world*]

Hello . . . hello . . . Who is this talking? Is this America? It dont sound like your voice, it sounds sad. Oh, it's Mr. The-Fellow-with-money. I thought it was somebody that was awful blue and dejected. Now quit crying and tell me how things are over there. Oh, they are terrible, are they?

Yes, I heard that Sinclair was nominated. I heard that in Siberia. That's the place they send all the rich men in Russia. Yes, I know we send 'em to the U. S. Senate. Its about the same thing.

Do you live in Cal? Oh, you dont. Well what are you

howling about? The stock market's gone to what? Spell it. H as in Huey. E as in the third letter of Huey and L as in Long and another L as in Long.

The market's gone, so the country's gone to the dogs? Well do the 119 million people that dont deal on the market — do they know that the market has gone to the dogs? Well, I would tell 'em if I was you.

Do you know what the old Stock Exchange in Leningrad is Now? It's a rest room . . . rest room, no, not pest house. You are thinking of ours.

Oh, Maine went Democratic, did it? Well, Maine is a small State. Oh, but as Maine goes, so went the Nation. How about A.A.L. — American Liberty League? There was headlines in the Russian papers about that, it said it was formed to give the capitalists some liberty.

Oh, it's blowed up already?

Well, just what is your grievances, Mr. Man-with-Money? Oh, you don't know where to invest it so you will be sure of a good return?

So that is it, the principal problem is what can you do with your money? Well, I been in many a country since I left home and I have heard many of their problems, but this one, "What can I do with my money?" is a unique problem. Every nation in the world would give a right leg to have that same thing wrong with 'em.

Well, I wouldent take it so hard if I was you. Maby Mr. Roosevelt will help you invest it . . . Oh, that's what you are afraid of?

Wait a minute, I cant stand this wailing. Hello, operator, put me on with a man without anything. Oh, there are plenty of 'em. Hello, this is old Will talking over in London. How's things over home anyhow?

No so bad . . . Oh, you mean you are getting along pretty good? And a mighty good chance of things picking up. By golly, what do you know about that!

I just talked to a rich fellow and he said things were terrible. He must be standing there by the phone, you can recognize him because he is moaning. Tell him England, the first country to recover, has the highest income tax rate of anybody in the world.

Tell him this too, that all their big men never lost confidence in England. They bet on England to win and ours are betting on our country to lose.

Tell him if I had some citizenship papers to hand out for our country, I could sign up everybody I have met.

SEPTEMBER 23, 1934 [*aboard* SS Île de France]

You know the American business man or traveler from home is a queer duck.

All over Europe and a couple of days ago on the boat this is all I heard, "I tell you I am afraid of things at home, it dont look good to me."

Well, for the last couple of days the market has picked up and todays news said the strikers went back to work. Now they are going around the boat grinning like possums. Imagine people whose whole idea of our country is gained from what it does every day in a stock market!

SEPTEMBER 30, 1934

The greatest aid that I know of that any could give the world today would be a correct definition of "Liberty."

Everybody is running around in a circle announcing that somebody's pinched their "Liberty."

Now what might be one classes "Liberty" might be another classes "poison."

I guess absolute "Liberty" couldent mean anything but that anybody can do anything they want to anytime they want to. Well any half wit can tell you that wouldent work.

So the question arises, "How much liberty can I get and get away with it?" Well, you can get no more than you give.

Thats my definition, but you got perfect "Liberty" to work out your own, so get in.

OCTOBER 11, 1934

Say the Republicans have turned the coming election into a real "youth movement." Just signed up for the coming society hop those ex-White House co-eds, Mrs. Benjamin Harrison, Mrs. Theodore Roosevelt, Mrs. William Howard Taft, Mrs. Calvin Coolidge and Mrs. Herbert Hoover. And nothing is any more gratifying to America than to welcome back into the fold all those gracious and sturdy American women. Funny thing about the White House, it wears down the most hardy of our men folks, but the women seem to thrive on it.

By the way this is Mrs. Franklyn Roosevelts birthday. I wish I knew where she was today, I would send her a message of good wishes as I am very fond of her. So here is a kind of blanket good wish to all of 'em, and Mrs. Woodrow Wilson. Sure you should all keep up your political affiliations and public interests. Don't retire. We want you to keep on living.

OCTOBER 19, 1934

Hoover Dam (thats no typographical error) grows a foot high a day. That sounds like Oklahoma weeds.

One old boy got fired from down in there the other day and as he walked out he got on a high peek and declared, "I hope it leaks." That sounds like a rich Republican wish to the New Deal.

NOVEMBER 7, 1934

The Republicans have had a saying for some time: "The Roosevelt honeymoon is over."

They were mighty poor judges of a love sick couple. Why he and the people have got a real love match and it looks like it would run for at least six years.

If there is one thing the Republican Party has got to learn it is that you cant get votes by just denouncing. You got to offer some plan of your own. They only had one platform: "elect us and maby we can think of something to do after we get in but up to now we havent thought of it. But give us a chance, we may."

NOVEMBER 8, 1934

In the heat of the moment, they have kicked out some awful good Republicans. And then, too, too big a victory aint so good. We need quite a few in there just as detectives, or watchdogs.

Then too you want to remember that an awful lot of these Democratic voters this time were really at heart

Republicans. They can revert back to type mighty quick, so dont rub it in, boys, for there aint any finer folks living than a Republican that votes the Democratic ticket.

NOVEMBER 11, 1934 [*Gulf radio broadcast*]

A friend passed away since I talked with you last Sunday night, and I wouldent feel right if I dident say a few words about him. I cant be eloquent and I am not worthy of doing it but I will try and make up in sincerity and feeling what I lack in words.

When you have heard of somebody since childhood and then as you grew up and met him, and become to know him, and to like him, and to see him become almost a tradition, then see him pass, right when it should have been the useful years of his life, well it kinder gets you.

He had been ill but was feeling more hopeful. But Tuesday morning last about Seven he started having acute pains and as the day went on they got worse. They called in what little medical help they had but it was feared he was beyond human aid. By nightfall, just as the sun was setting, he breathed his last. This gallant old figure, that had been loved by many, feared by many, had gone to where there is no returning. All that was mortal of the *Republican Party* had left this earth. He passed away because he wanted to live like a pioneer, he couldent change with modern civilization.

The word spread like wildfire. The news was flashed to the four corners of our land. From the nostrils of every static radio in home or jail belched forth the news, "The king is dead, The King is dead."

It struck us like a thunderbolt. We knew that he was ill. We knew that he had never fully recovered from that stroke which he had in October 1929 — a paralytic stroke brought on by loss of marginal blood. That stroke laid him low. And it happened just when he was at the heighth of his career. Just when things looked the brightest for him. Just when he was bragging of being Oh, so "rugged." With not a dark cloud (that he could see) on his horizon, he was made practically bed ridden. It was the unexpectedness of it that struck him and his immediate family. He had been warned. But not by any of his doctors or close friends. He had been warned by outsiders that he was living too high, and that it was liable to bring on a fluttering heart.

But he scoffed at them. What do they know about me and my health (they are just jealous of my ruddy condition). They cant match my power and they are envious. Why I will keep on living like this forever. I have solved the problem of power, its mass energy, its life everlasting. And then came the dawn.

But you must give the old boy credit. When the blow hit him that bright shiny October day of '29, with no climatic warning, he lived up to all political traditions.

What did he do?

He said it wasent his fault, and it wasent his fault. It was everybodys fault, it was your fault, it was my fault, it was the Lord's fault. He just stepped in and said, "Wait a minute. How long has this been going on? This living on a dog eat dog basis. We will stop this thing right now and give you folks a chance to reorganize and redeem yourselves."

Now here is where the mistake was made. Had the Republicans held a clinic at that very moment and decided, "Boys, our patient is sick. He has got acute appendicitis. Now of course an operation is going to cost us all something. We are all going to have to chip in. It will take part of what we have. But it may save us in the long run. There is a change coming in our lives and we cant do the things we have always done. We can no more ask for the same conditions to continue than we can ask for our youth to continue."

Now had that been done this obituary notice that was posted on every cross road last Tuesday Night might not have happened. But instead they decided at the clinic that it wasent really appendicitis, that it was cramp colic, and that a strong healthy man like he was could throw it off. That he had always been healthy and there was no reason he should be sick. And the only thing to do was just to let nature take its course. That they had always come out of these cramp colics without having to give up anything and there was no reason why this one should be different. That was as I say from October 29 to November 7, 1932.

On November 8, 1932, nature took its course and the patient had another stroke. They still said they wouldent have to operate. They rushed with the ice bags again but not with the knife. They still contended that they were right and the disease was wrong.

Well in an argument with a disease, be it physical or

economic, you better at least let it have a hearing. But in spite of his pain, in spite of his groans, his doctors, and his whole family maintained that he was "fundamentally sound." That he had never been operated on in his life and had lived this long and that they could see no reason to think that his same life's program and schedule should not go on as it always had.

Well, he had his third and last stroke last Tuesday and he went to his maker, a physical wreck but "fundamentally sound." And on his tombstone it says, "Here lies a rugged individual, but he wasent rugged enough to compete with a Democrat."

Now we come to that Great question of reincarnation. Does the soul return in another body? I believe it will. I dont know what animal he will come back in. It wont be an elephant, it will be something with much less humility. It will be a very domestic animal, an animal more in the nature of a dog. It will have faith, its whole soul will be consecrated to service.

And will this animal be needed?

He certainly will, for the Democrats by that time will have passed out through too much power. The Democrats could never stand power as long as the Republicans did. They are not used to it. They are getting "cocky" already and they only been in overnight. So the Republicans being the first to die, will be the first to come back. So lets say a good word for the deceased and ask him to be ready to move over in his grave.

The Democrats will be crawling in there with him pretty soon.

CHAPTER SIXTEEN

The Only Fleas Weighing Over 100 Pounds

JANUARY 1, 1935

There is a big demand in this country for a return to "normalcy." But there is no two people in the whole 120 million that can agree just when "normalcy" was.

Normalcy, to every one of us, was the year that we were doing the best. In other words normalcy was our peak year. I imagine that we would be surprised if we knew the amount of people that wouldent mind seeing a war come on as during the last one was their "normalcy."

A man that's getting more on relief than he ever got working, why these days right now are "normalcy" to him.

College professors in Government work, this is their "normalcy." Men who love to make speeches, offer 90 percent criticism and ten percent remedy, this year is their "normalcy."

So when you say let's return to normalcy, you want to ask, "Whose normalcy," mine or yours?

Normalcy with the Republicans was when they were

in; normalcy with the Democrats are these glorious days we are going through, and "going through is right, Brother, we are going through with a lot."

Normalcy with Hoover was '28. Normalcy with Roosevelt started with '32. Normalcy with Al Capone was around '30 and '31. Normalcy with Huey Long is right now, today. He never was agoing so good. Normalcy with me was when I owed nothing and paid no income tax.

JANUARY 12, 1935

Never a time in our lifetime was money as scared as it is now. Even during the war when folks were asked to shovel it out they dident hesitate, but then they felt that they were able to keep on making it, but now there is a doubt, and they want to hang onto it as long as they can. We are getting two fairly well defined schools of thought on what is ones obligation to another.

Mr. Roosevelt has a very liberal idea on the subject. He thinks that there has to be a more generous feeling toward those who are in need, and if it cant be arrived at by persuasion, he will arrange some other way of making each meet their share.

JANUARY 19, 1935

I sure would hate to be running for something and have somebody dig back through old papers and confront me with all the nut things that I have shown my ignorance on.

You see conditions and events change so fast, that what is passable today, is ridiculous tomorrow.

FEBRUARY 17, 1935

See by todays papers Mr. Townsend appeared before the Senate Committee and they had a lot of fun and laughter at his plan. Well they can have some fun with the amount, but they cant have much fun with the idea of paying a pension. You see its not just some idealistic cranks, or Bolsheviki idea. All the rest of the world are doing it but us.

We thought we had a better idea. We called it "Poor Farm," and everybody that could afford it, or had any political influence, put their old relatives there. Now Townsend may have to take 25 or 15 percent of his original ideas, but the Senators are not going to laugh themselves out of paying an old age pension.

APRIL 7, 1935

Legislatures are kinder like animals in a zoo. You cant do anything about 'em. All you can do is just stand and watch 'em.

But "man" is still the main animal. You put a bunch of 'em in the legislature and he can think of more funny tricks to do than the same amount of monkeys in a cage will.

We cuss the lawmakers, but I notice we are always perfectly willing to share in any of these vast sums of money that they spend. We say its wrong and unsound but we dont refuse to take it. We say the government is nutty and throwing away money. But anytime any is thrown our way we have never dodged it.

The general contention is that nobody is spending any

money but the government. Well an awful lot of businesses are doing better than they have for the last three or four years. Newspaper advertising has leaped, subscriptions have gone up.

Yet the editorials all say Roosevelt is a — DUD. That the thing cant go on, that the government is spending all the money. But they are doing better than they have in years on the Go. money.

It shows the "absolute honesty" of the press, it shows that the editorial policy of the papers *are not* influenced by the man who is responsible for bringing 'em in all the business.

You know you figure it out and its a peculiar state of affairs. Everybody that is doing better, or making money, has got it in for Roosevelt. But he dont seem to realize he is doing better on the money that Roosevelt is spending.

Now we all know that the Government spending all the money, thats not a good state of affairs to exist. A country is in bad shape when there aint nobody spending money but the Government.

Well if the government is throwing the money away, the only thing I see is for the ones that they are throwing it to (outside of those that absolutely need it) why, *have them refuse to take it.* Just say, no, its government money and its tainted. And I dont believe in the government spending all this money and hence I dont take any part of it.

You say, "No, you have paid this out to the people to eat, and they have come to see my pictures with it. I refuse to accept the money. Its government money and I dont believe in the government spending this money, so I am not going to take it."

Here is a man that wants to pay his loan at the bank. "I dont believe in the government spending all this money, so I am not going to take it. I will just carry the fellow myself. I made the loan and its me that should lose."

But you havent heard that, have you?

There is not a person in America that has received a dollar no matter where it come from that hasent grabbed it. It might have been paid out to relieve a starving child, but if it reached us we were the starving child.

So the only thing I see is for the fellow that dont believe in all this spending is to not participate in the receiving of any of it.

Dont be too critical of the present plan as long as you are living on the loot from it.

May 27, 1935

Poor old "New Deal" she went to bat three times today with the Supreme Court pitching and she struck out each time.

May 29, 1935

We are funny people. Business men have howled from every luncheon table the evils of the whole NRA. Then all at once the Supreme Court says, "The bridle is off, boys, from this day on every man for himself." Now the same men are rushing back to the banquet tables and unoccupied microphones and shouting, "Wages must be maintained." "Cut throat competition must be curbed." "Child labor is wrong." "The sweat shop must not return." You just cant please some people.

Say just talk to some small merchants, or druggists, get them to tell you whats going on now in the price cutting, chiselling, and conniving lines. Its terrible to have a law telling you you got to do something. But you aint going to do it unless there is.

June 3, 1935

Well the old NRA is out to stay. And we had a celebration. All the big strong Republican papers, why you would have thought it was Armistice Day. Big Business threw confetti and cut salaries and just had a great time. They all hollered, "At last we are back to the constitution."

They going to try to retain the best features of NRA by persuasion. Hours and wages.

You got to admit Roosevelt is trying to get a semblance of fairness. But they wouldent even do it by law, so this scheme looks doubtful.

Roosevelt thinks there should be a law saying how long you can work a man and the lowest sum you can pay him.

The Court says you can't do that. Well that's a pretty big question. If there is no way of the under dog getting assistance by law, why things wont look any too rosy for the under dog.

The other side says, "We have got where we are by this set of laws, so why change 'em. Let the Constitution alone."

But here is something they forget. They can rightfully say, "We got where we are by these laws," but there is a lot of folks that havent got anywhere under 'em, and the prospects aint too bright to get any further. So they might not be so averse to some light changes in the Constitution. So it all gets back to just "How good has the Constitution been to you?" And nobody can answer that question but yourself.

JUNE 9, 1935

The Republicans say that Roosevelt's schemes are all to "Reform somebody." That for him to let 'em recover first and then they will reform. Roosevelt wants to know why they cant reform first! Now that's the whole thing in a nutshell (I mean it was in a nutshell up to the time I uttered it).

Now here's another way of putting it. Roosevelt wants recovery to start at the bottom. In other words by a system of high taxes he wants business to help the little fellow to get started, get some work, and then pay business back by buying things when he is at work.

Business says, "Let everything alone and quit monkeying with it and trying schemes and we will get it going for you, and as we prosper why naturally the workers will prosper." That's what business says.

One wants recovery to start from the bottom and the other wants it to start from the top. I dont know which is right.

I dont think either one of 'em know what its all about. Both sides are doing nothing now but looking to the next election. Well, they don't have to give that a thought. If sentiment at that time is strong enough against Roosevelt, Republicans can nominate Little Shirley Temple and win with her.

In this country people dont vote — *for* — they vote — *against*.

In 1936 the vote will either be FOR or AGAINST Mr. Roosevelt. The other fellow wont cut any figure. And the whole thing will depend upon conditions.

These denouncing orators should remember every time they cuss a President, they lose friends. They may get applause from a partisan audience but we still think its the highest office in the whole world.

So any — denouncer — no matter which side he is on loses more votes than he gains.

Dont argue and get mad over these problems. Conditions and not oratory will settle it.

June 19, 1935

At the great San Diego Worlds Fair yesterday Mr. Hoover received a tremendous ovation. There is no country in the world where a person changes from a hero to a goat, and a goat to a hero, or visa versa, as they do with us. And all through no change of them, the change is always us.

Its not our public men that you cant put your finger on, its our public.

We are the only fleas weighing over 100 pounds. We dont know what we want, but we are ready to bite somebody to get it.

JULY 4, 1935

That liberty we got 159 years ago was a great thing. Never was as much politics indulged in under the guise of "Freedom and liberty."

They was 5 percent what George Washington did, and 95 percent what the speaker intended to do. What this country needs on July the Fourth is not more "Liberty or more freedom." Its a Roman candle that only shoots out of one end.

So Long

In the summer of 1935 Will flipped a coin to see if he would take a plane trip with Wiley Post to Alaska and perhaps on around the world.

"See, I win," he said to Mrs. Rogers.

This meant that he took the trip.

The plane crashed on a lonely tundra fifteen miles north of Point Barrow in Alaska, killing both of them.

Perhaps Will did win. Certainly the United States lost. This was particularly true the following summer when the Presidential nominating conventions met. And it has been true ever since.